Contexts in Literature

Contemporary Poetry:
Poets and Poetry
since 1990

Ian Brinton

Series editor: Adrian Barlow

CAMBRIDGE
UNIVERSITY PRESS

CAMBRIDGE UNIVERSITY PRESS
Cambridge, New York, Melbourne, Madrid, Cape Town, Singapore,
São Paulo, Delhi

Cambridge University Press
The Edinburgh Building, Cambridge CB2 8RU, UK

www.cambridge.org
Information on this title: www.cambridge.org/9780521712484

First published 2009

Printed in the United Kingdom at the University Press, Cambridge

A catalogue record for this publication is available from the British Library

ISBN 978-0-521-71248-4 paperback

Editorial management: Gill Stacey

Cover illustration: Joy at death itself 5, 2002
Indian ink, gouache and crayon on paper
152 x 102cm
Courtesy of the artist, Ian Friend, and Andrew Baker Art Dealer, Brisbane.

Contents

Introduction

The aim of this book is to offer an introduction to the world of contemporary poetry, that is, poetry written and published since 1990, and the central image will be that of a voyage of discovery. The two companions whom I have chosen for this venture are Ruth Padel and Peter Robinson and I strongly urge readers to obtain the two texts to which I shall be making reference throughout the journey, Ruth Padel's *The Poem and the Journey* and Peter Robinson's *Talk about Poetry – Conversations on the Art*. Ruth Padel calls the act of reading poetry 'a necessary art' which enriches what goes on inside us, fortifying our inwardness; her book offers a close reading of sixty modern poems. Peter Robinson's book is a collection of eleven interviews or 'conversations' about writing poetry.

This brief guide is about the act of reading complex poetry and coming to terms with the immediate difficulties it presents. With that in mind, it might be worth considering the following basic rules:

- do not expect a poem's complexities to be understood at a quick glance
- we share a common language and need to look carefully at what words mean
- sometimes we can feel the powerful emotion in a piece of poetry without being able to say immediately precisely how it works.

One other central piece of advice is a quotation from T.S. Eliot: 'We learn what poetry is – if we ever learn – from reading it.'

Peter Robinson says, in the first of his *Conversations*, 'Poems, for me, come out of the circumstances of life', and in an earlier book of criticism about poems and poets, *In the Circumstances*, he suggests that poetry is 'a response to other lives and the otherness of those lives'. In the second of his *Conversations*, Robinson is asked about 'silences' or 'those moments when language falters or fails' and his reply is important:

> Yes, silences are places where poetry starts and stops, where taboo subjects wait to be touched on. If there's something that can't be said, poetry might try to make it sayable, or find a way of pointing to what remains to be intuited.

Although the circumstances of life, personal experience, may well be the starting-point for a poet, Robinson also emphasises how 'poems need to stand relatively alone' and he calls upon his experiences as a university teacher in Japan to emphasise this:

> In formal gardens here they have a bamboo device that sends a drop of water into a pond at intervals just to emphasise the silence.

This idea and its relation to a haiku by the Japanese poet, Matsuo Basho, is further explored in Part 5 (pages 114–116).

Robinson also suggests that inspiration comes from ordinary events and occasions. The truth of this can be seen in Barry MacSweeney's poem 'I Looked Down on a Child Today' (Part 3, page 76), written after witnessing a fatal road accident in Newcastle-on-Tyne.

There are challenges to tradition which occupy the centre ground of today's poetry world and they involve the increasing use of the Internet for publication and the arrival of print-on-demand books from Salt Publishing and Shearsman Books. The Poetry Society now embraces new media with a brand new series of podcasts. As is suggested by Tom Chivers, director of *Penned in the Margins,* the podcast can be streamed online or downloaded onto a portable media player.

The reference to podcasts brings to the fore the connection between poetry and music. Ruth Padel recalls once hearing the Scottish poet, John Burnside, saying 'When I read a poem that turns me on, it isn't accessible at once. There's a mystery to it. What draws you in is the music.' In his third *Conversation*, Robinson is asked about the difference between writing poetry and writing prose; his reply refers to the condition of music:

> The difference, as far as I am concerned, lies in the distinction that some have noted between composing and writing. Poetry, as I understand it, cannot be just written. It has to form itself as rhythmical units, preferably in the head, sometimes on paper. These rhythmical units, phrases or sentences, with or without an enjambed turn or two, are intolerant of 'filler': they can't be mashed into whatever grammatical shape I happen to fancy. Nor do they incline themselves to fit into a predetermined stanza-form. Finding the shape and the grammar involves discovering what the phrases mean to say, where they need to go, what they're telling me.

The poet is suggesting here that he needs to listen, to be attentive to what is being sounded or, as he puts it later in the same conversation, 'learning to recognise words making themselves felt, and developing means for responding to them'. There is an echo here of Charles Tomlinson's poem, 'Aesthetic', from his early volume *The Necklace* (1955), which announced a new voice in English poetry at that time:

> Reality is to be sought, not in concrete,
> But in space made articulate

The idea of giving voice to 'space' suggests that the gaps between things are what give the objects definition, just as the space between musical notes is central to the whole structure. Music is made up not only of notes, but of the spaces and gaps between notes. A little like the Basho haiku referred to in Part 5, sound and silence both take their force from being placed side by side. John Cage, the American composer, went so far as to create a composition which defied the expected routines of what music should consist of. *4'33"*, written in 1952, was a musical 'happening' where a formally-dressed pianist went on to the stage, sat at a grand piano, opened the lid and sat quietly for four minutes and thirty-three seconds before rising, bowing to the audience and leaving. *4'33"* isn't of course a silent composition at all. Although the pianist makes as little sound as possible, just the occasional turning over of the sheets of music, the audience's attention is inevitably upon the sounds both within and outside the auditorium. The audience learns to attend to those noises, which might include their own memories of noise, which are routinely taken for granted and given no real attention.

In this context it is worth noting that the late 20th-century English poet, Anthony Barnett, two of whose pieces of writing are in Part 3 (see pages 102–103), suggested in an interview in 1992 that 'what you play acts upon the silence, determines the nature, the sound of the silence which follows'. Talking about the trumpet player Leo Smith, he says 'Each sound phrase has its corresponding silent phrase'. Silence isn't of course poetry but it is the ground out of which poetry grows – and this thought is delicately caught by the New York poet, William Bronk, in 'Her Singing' (1956):

> As trees draw outward from the rooted ground
> from trunk to branch to twig to stem to leaves,
> her song was as she might have drawn upon
> the air a tree, and it stood still.

It is the music of the song which creates the sculpted stillness of the tree out of the insubstantial air.

As we make our way through the challenging worlds of contemporary poetry, it will be sensible to take the advice of Peter Riley, a poet and critic whose work has spanned the 1960s to the present moment. His early poem, 'Introitus', was written in the late 1960s but was only published by Shearsman in a volume of *Uncollected Writings* in 2007. It appears in full in Part 3 (see page 101). The title of the poem means 'an entrance' and refers to words sung by a choir in church as the priest approaches the altar. Riley's years living on the coast in Hastings had taught him about the difficulty of walking on shingle and about the care needed in order to make progress:

> To walk effectively on shingle you have to
> lean forwards so you'd fall if you didn't push
> your feet back from a firm step down and
> back sharp forcing the separate ground
> to consolidate underneath you, with a marked
> flip as you lift each foot, scattering
> stones behind, gaining momentum.

This act of walking is an interesting metaphor for the reading of poetry.

How this book is organised

Part 1: Approaching contemporary poetry

Part 1 is a survey of the background to contemporary poetry. It looks at the influence of T.S. Eliot, as well as Thomas Hardy, and charts the growth of modern ideas about poetry. There is also a section on poetry publishing, focusing particularly on the continuing growth of website publishing, and a brief overview of key political events since 1990 as a context for recent poetry.

Part 2: Approaching the texts

Part 2 considers different areas of contemporary poetry including sections on women's poetry, contemporary scenes of war, poetry in translation and Black poetry.

Part 3: Texts and extracts

Part 3 contains texts and extracts which illustrate the key themes found elsewhere in the book.

Part 4: Critical approaches

Part 4 examines some different ways in which critics have approached the subject of contemporary poetry.

Part 5: How to write about contemporary poetry

Part 5 offers a guideline of how to write about poetry and how to compare poems with each other.

Part 6: Resources

Part 6 contains guidance for further reading and a list of significant websites. There is also a glossary and index.

1 | Approaching contemporary poetry

- What is so central about T.S. Eliot's influence on contemporary poetry?

- What is important about 20th-century American poetry in the development of poetry in Britain?

- Why were the 'poetry wars' of the 1970s important?

- What are the major differences between 'closed / fixed form' and 'open form' poetry?

- What impact has Internet publishing had on poetry readership?

In the beginning: T.S. Eliot and Dante

One of the great figures whose presence towers over the development of modern poetry in Britain is T.S. Eliot, whose poem *The Waste Land*, published in 1922, shocked and bewildered many contemporary readers. In a review for the *Manchester Guardian*, October 1923, Charles Powell suggested that the ordinary reader would make nothing of the poem: 'The thing is a mad medley.' But what he saw as a medley, an earlier reviewer for the *New York Tribune* had seen as 'the agonised outcry of a sensitive romanticist drowning in a sea of jazz'. In the *London Mercury* a reviewer complained that he had read Eliot's poem several times but was still unable to make head or tail of it, whilst an unsigned but sympathetic review in the *Times Literary Supplement*, November 1923, suggested that *The Waste Land* is a 'collection of flashes' which, like a **collage**, seem to be a 'complete expression of this poet's vision of modern life'. The reviewer went on to say:

> We have here range, depth, and beautiful expression. What more is necessary to a great poem? This vision is singularly complex and in all its labyrinths utterly sincere. It is the mystery of life that it shows two faces, and we know of no other modern poet who can more adequately and movingly reveal to us the inextricable tangle of the sordid and the beautiful that make up life.

T.S. Eliot was born and educated in America but spent most of his working life in England. His work is steeped in the European cultural tradition and *The Waste Land* is filled with references to French poetry, Shakespeare, Ovid, Arthurian legend and Wagner. A central influence on Eliot was the Italian poet Dante (1265–1321), whose long poem *Inferno* describes the poet's journey through the nine circles of Hell, guided by the spirit of the Latin poet Virgil.

Dante's vision of the enormous suffering of the damned, accompanied by their searing self-analysis, has had a major influence on modern poetry. This can be seen in Ciaran Carson's translation of Canto III (2002), where the enormous and frightening picture of lost souls, 'grey people', is seen in terms of

> outlandish tongues, and accents doloroso,
> > howls, shrieks, grunts, gasps, bawls,
> > a never-ending, terrible crescendo,
>
> rising to vast compulsory applause,
> > revolving like sand or locusts in a storm,
> > turning the air black as funereal gauze.

The lifelong importance of Dante to Eliot is evident in the text of a lecture he gave to the Italian Institute in July 1950, in which he acknowledged that the debt he owed to the Italian poet was of the kind 'which goes on accumulating, the kind which is not the debt of one period or another of one's life'. Eliot reminded his audience of his vision in *The Waste Land* of city clerks trooping over London Bridge from the railway station to their offices:

> A crowd flowed over London Bridge, so many,
> I had not thought death had undone so many.
> Sighs, short and infrequent, were exhaled,
> And each man fixed his eyes before his feet.
> Flowed up the hill and down King William Street,
> To where Saint Mary Woolnoth kept the hours
> With a dead sound on the final stroke of nine.

Eliot was concerned that his readers should recognise precisely where he had obtained this image, from Canto III of *The Inferno*, and gave references in his notes 'in order to make the reader who recognised the allusion, know that I meant him to recognise it, and know that he would have missed the point if he did not recognise it'. Some twenty years after *The Waste Land,* Eliot attempted an equivalent to a Dante canto in *Four Quartets* – in 'Little Gidding' a hallucinatory meeting during a World War Two air-raid has the dramatic vividness of one of Dante's confrontations with the souls of the dead who are in Hell:

> In the uncertain hour before the morning
> > Near the ending of interminable night
> > At the recurrent end of the unending
> After the dark dove with the flickering tongue
> > Had passed below the horizon of his homing
> > While the dead leaves still rattled on like tin
> Over the asphalt where no other sound was

> Between three districts whence the smoke arose
> I met one walking, loitering and hurried
> As if blown towards me like the metal leaves
> Before the urban dawn wind unresisting.

In his 1950 lecture, Eliot commented upon the difficulty he had had writing this section of the poem:

> It was not simply that I was limited to the Dantesque type of imagery, simile and figure of speech. It was chiefly that in this very bare and austere style, in which every word has to be 'functional', the slightest vagueness or imprecision is immediately noticeable.

Concluding his talk to the Italian Institute, Eliot suggested that reading Dante became a constant reminder to any poet 'of the obligation to explore, to find words for the inarticulate, to capture those feelings which people can hardly even feel, because they have no words for them'.

The importance of Dante to contemporary poets

The enduring importance of Dante's poetry is highlighted by the number of translations of *Inferno* which have appeared over the last twenty years. The most notable include those by Steve Ellis, the Irish poet Ciaran Carson, J.G. Nichols and Sean O'Brien. In addition, there have been two outstanding translations in America by Robert Pinsky and Michael Palma. Seamus Heaney's continued fascination with the dramatic immediacy of Dante's vision can be seen in 'Ugolino', the poem which closes *Field Work* and is also evident in 'The Crossing' (see Part 3, page 70), as well as in the imagery of circularity and danger which informs the title poem of his 2006 collection, *District and Circle* (see Part 3, page 72). In the latter poem, the siren-like call from the underground acts as an eerie opening to a poem that was written as a sequence of sonnets in the aftermath of the London bombings of July 2005:

> Tunes from a tin whistle underground
> Curled up a corridor I'd be walking down
> To where I knew I was always going to find
> My watcher on the tiles, cap by his side,
> His fingers perked, his two eyes eyeing me
> In an unaccusing look I'd not avoid,
> Or not just yet, since both were out to see
> For ourselves.

The opening lines of the second sonnet in Heaney's sequence conjure up the labyrinthine structures depicted by the 18th-century artist Piranesi. Piranesi's

Imaginary Prisons is a series of sixteen prints revealing enormous subterranean vaults and stairs:

> Posted, eyes front, along the dreamy ramparts
> Of escalators ascending and descending
> To a monotonous slight rocking in the works,
> We were moved along, upstanding.

Much of Heaney's poem revolves around feelings of guilt and retribution, images of which have become more haunting as the threat of terrorist attacks has grown during the first decade of the 21st century.

The American reaction: William Carlos Williams and R.F. Langley

Whilst Dante's influence continues to be one of the cornerstones of European culture, it is also worthwhile to consider the American reaction to T.S. Eliot's leanings towards the old European world. The contemporary poetry which appears in this volume has been influenced by both Eliot's tradition and that of the 20th-century American modernist poets. There was a clear sense to some poets that Eliot had turned his back on what was happening in his home country, the New World. One of the major 20th-century American poets, William Carlos Williams (1883–1963), claimed in his autobiographical work that *The Waste Land* had 'wiped out our world as if an atom bomb had been dropped upon it':

> Critically Eliot returned us to the classroom just at the moment when
> I felt that we were on the point of an escape to matters much closer
> to the essence of a new art form itself – rooted in the locality which
> should give it fruit.
>
> (*Autobiography of a Poet*, 1951)

Williams registered his regret that a craftsman as fine as Eliot should turn his back on American poetry and lose contact with the 'locality', the 'western dialect', the American common scene and the sounds of colloquial American English. This is central to an understanding of one important strand of contemporary poetry: an awareness of the value of ordinary moments and the emotional importance of the everyday. For Williams, Eliot's treason was losing contact with the accomplishments of American technology and industry, as he saw it:

> American plumbing, American shoes, American bridges, indexing
> systems, locomotives, printing presses, city buildings, farm
> implements and a thousand other things that have become notable in
> the world.
>
> (*Contact*, Spring 1921)

It is no surprise that Williams's most-quoted phrase, from a short poem in 1927 and later used in near-heraldic fashion at the opening of his most ambitious work, *Paterson* (Book 1, 1946), should be:

Say it! No ideas but in things.

Precise language

The importance of precision as a register of human emotion, a register of how our lives are defined in relation to a world of objects, can be seen in the poem 'The Tooth' by Robert Minhinnick (see Part 3, page 92). Minhinnick visited the Amariya bomb shelter in Iraq where four hundred people were burned to death during an American bombing raid in 1991:

    to pick the tooth
Of a child like a rice grain
From the ash.

It is the particularity, the small exactness of the object, which conveys the horror to us. It is the reference to vulnerability, 'the tooth / Of a child', which adds the turn of the screw and it is the reference to 'a rice grain' which raises for us the haunting spectre of world poverty and growing food shortages.

In contrast to Eliot's submersion in European cultural history, Williams concentrated upon the small individual moments which go to make up our perceptions. In 1923 he wrote the eight lines which could almost have been written in the last decade of the 20th century:

so much depends
upon

a red wheel
barrow

glazed with rain
water

beside the white
chickens

Catherine Belsey suggests that this poem offers the clearly defined colours and shapes of things referred to; it seems to transmit the things themselves to our imagination. It is as though 'so much depends' upon their solid existence in a substantial world:

And yet, if we look again, there is another way to read this short,
simple text. The red and white in this poem are unqualified, and thus

bright, shiny, 'glazed'. If this is a farmyard, it is one without shadows, or mud. Indeed, we might more readily 'see' a toy wheelbarrow, or a scene in a children's picture book. The poem seems to depict an innocence and purity not to be found on any real farm and, at least according to one possible interpretation, 'so much depends' on our ability to conceive of that lost but childlike world. Here the rhythms are simplicity itself, each short 'verse' repeating with minor variations the metrical pattern of the one before. On this reading, the red wheelbarrow of this poem issues from language, not from the world of things.

(Poststructuralism, A Very Short Introduction, 2002)

In poetry, images present us with pictures in words and they allow us to see clearly what the poet has in mind. Often they seem to be chosen as representations of some 'truth' or 'meaning'. In this context it is worth bearing in mind the clear sense of an object *being there* in the red wheelbarrow poem. After all, does it have to *mean* something? Isn't it enough that we can simply *see* it?

R.F. Langley, school-teacher and poet (see 'Man Jack', Part 3, page 83), responded to an interview question about images. His interviewer commented that 'there seems little of what many poetry readers might think of as imagery in these poems. Would it be true to say that your poetry does not operate in this kind of way at all?' Langley replied:

> Well, if by imagery you mean a concern for the visual, I'd like to feel my poetry had it all the time. And I do also think that I am very aware of the metaphorical, metaphysical aspect…I would tend to prefer 'The Red Wheelbarrow' sort of imagery where there isn't that sort of metaphorical foisting. There's just an opening up to what is there in front. With things mattering about it.

(Angel Exhaust, 1996)

Ruth Padel describes how she talked to a Greek van-driver whose vehicle had the sign 'METAPHORS' on its side. When she asked the man what he did he replied 'Taking something from one place to another,' which is of course what a metaphor does. Metaphors compare things, they say what one thing is like in terms of another. Padel refers to Aristotle's example of a metaphor: 'The ship ploughed the sea' in terms of how the word 'plough' transfers the associated meanings of agricultural work and growth to the sense of voyage over the ocean. She points out that when you say something is 'like' something else you are registering that it is not actually that thing: 'metaphor separates as well as joining its two things, two worlds'.

In the same interview referred to above, Langley talks about the importance of these different worlds. He talks about standing under a tree in Suffolk for an hour and a half, not moving:

> I thought that was an interesting experience: to be alone and perfectly still. As soon as you move things take on meaning, don't they? Things become things that you've got to step round or walk over or something. They instantly become part of your map, as it were. Whereas if you stand absolutely still, then they might not be part of any map at all. You 'see' the place when you haven't got any designs on it …

The purpose behind using metaphors is to give meaning to the inanimate: we are surrounded by objects which say everything about who we are and what we do. Walter Benjamin, the German literary critic and philosopher, called the inanimate 'time filled by the presence of the now' which highlights for us the immediacy of the things which surround us. Eliot's *The Waste Land* is a literary collage where the fragments of different cultures are cut and pasted together. Their personal or talismanic importance to the poet is highlighted when he says 'These fragments I have shored against my ruins'. 'Shored' is defined as 'a piece of timber or iron set obliquely against the side of a building as a support when it is in danger of falling'; this suggests that the objects, the things, which Eliot has collected are the props, the supports, that can keep him going: they maintain his sanity in a bewildering world.

George Oppen

George Oppen (1908–1984), a New York friend of William Carlos Williams, was an American poet who published a small volume of poems, *Discrete Series*, in 1934. He gave up writing poetry for a time when he became immersed in the world of politics during the troubled years of the American Depression. He started to write again in the 1950s and became one of the most moving, careful and sharply perceptive of American poets of the 20th century. The English poet Charles Tomlinson wrote an essay titled 'The Integrity of George Oppen', in which he referred to Oppen's work as 'sharing the walls and streets of ordinary living' and identified the territory of the American poet as being:

> … where the human faced the inanimate or the mechanical, shut in by buildings or behind car windows, and where poems might spring up with difficulty like seedlings between cracks in the pavement.
>
> (Introduction to Oppen's *Selected Poems*, 1990)

Oppen wrote about what the eye sees: his poetry is about the human vision which creates the human universe. He repeatedly asserts the importance of the small moments that make up the quality of life. This is especially true when he found himself faced with political and human disaster as in 'Time of the Missile', a poem from *The Materials* (1962):

I remember a square of New York's Hudson River glinting
    between warehouses.
Difficult to approach the water below the pier
Swirling, covered with oil the ship at the pier
A steel wall: tons in the water,

Width.
The hand for holding,
Legs for walking,
The eye *sees*! It floods in on us from here to Jersey tangled
    in the grey bright air!

Become the realm of nations.

My love, my love,
We are endangered
Totally at last. Look
Anywhere to the sight's limit: space
Which is viviparous:

Place of the mind
And eye. Which can destroy us,
Re-arrange itself, assert
Its own stone chain reaction.

The appalling presence of a nuclear vessel with its looming sense of threat is an image which has remained in our consciousness over the last forty-five years. In a letter from the same period, Oppen referred to his hatred of 'the stone universe'. He didn't mean to contemplate the possible end of the world as disguised in a political or topical poem, but he did want to suggest how these thoughts must be in everyone's minds 'with the threat of the missile right there'. He was very aware that we can never be free of the fear that any international agreement on the non-proliferation of atomic weapons might not be secure. The poem presents an inescapable presence, 'A steel wall: tons in the water', and juxtaposes this looming figure with the fragility of 'The hand for holding, / Legs for walking'. The melancholy cry 'My love, my love, / We are endangered / Totally at last' seems to echo the yearning request which Matthew Arnold put to his new wife on the cliffs of Dover in 'Dover Beach' (1849):

Ah, love, let us be true
To one another! for the world which seems
To lie before us like a land of dreams,
So various, so beautiful, so new,
Hath really neither joy, nor love, nor light,
Nor certitude, nor peace, nor help for pain,
And we are here as on a darkling plain
Swept with confused alarms of struggle and flight,
Where ignorant armies clash by night.

One can see the roots of modern poetry stretching back to the final words of Arnold's poem.

Oppen was a great admirer of another New York poet, Charles Reznikoff; he often referred to the two-line stanza in the latter's poem 'Jerusalem the Golden' (1934):

Among the heaps of brick and plaster lies
A girder, still itself among the rubbish.

(These two lines are explored further on page 21.) In a letter to his half-sister, Oppen wrote:

Likely he [Rezi] could mull along and tell you what he had in mind. But how other than with this image could he put into your mind so clearly the miracle of existence – the existence of things. It is only because the image hits so clear and sudden that the poem means what it means. I don't know that he could make it any clearer by talking about it.

(February 1959)

When Michael Davidson produced Oppen's *New Collected Poems* he commented on Oppen's compositional method, which involved a 'tendency to embed poems in the midst of a kind of textual rubble'. This image took on a particular moving intensity in 1968 in Oppen's forty-section poem 'Of Being Numerous'. There is a moment in Section 18 where compassion and outrage merge in response to President Lyndon Johnson's promotion of the Vietnam War:

It is the air of atrocity,
An event as ordinary
As a President.

A plume of smoke, visible at a distance
In which people burn.

The apparent ordinariness of the loss of human life has become increasingly evident in our own time, particularly through war and strife in Iraq and

Afghanistan. Oppen's distancing of the action in his image of 'A plume of smoke' directs us forward to the present when the reporting of the 21st-century Iraq War is in danger of inuring us to the atrocities committed day after day and only 'visible at a distance'.

Ezra Pound and Charles Tomlinson

Ezra Pound (1885–1972), the American-born poet who lived much of his life in London and Italy, was another powerful force in the development of 20th-century poetry. He was described by T.S. Eliot in his epigraph to *The Waste Land* as 'Il miglior fabbro' ('the better craftsman') after Pound had looked closely at the jumbled and confusing manuscript which was to become *The Waste Land*. Carving his way through the rhetorical confusion, much of which was a reflection of Eliot's acute mental distress, Pound shaped the poem. It was published as he directed. Eliot's epigraph dedicated to the skills of his fellow-American became a register of how much he owed to this larger-than-life figure.

The importance of Pound's influence on contemporary poets can be seen in Charles Tomlinson's account of studying English at Cambridge just after the Second World War. It is a fascinating personal document which says more about reading modern poetry than many theoretical studies of the subject. As with all good autobiographies it tells a story:

> A boy from the provinces, going up to read English at Cambridge in 1945, as I did, will have learned little of American poetry from his university teachers. None of them seemed to mention it. While still at grammar school, I had invested half a crown, that no longer extant coin, in a copy of the Sesame Books selection of Ezra Pound.
>
> (*Some Americans*, 1979)

Tomlinson goes on to tell us how struck he was by the 'cleanliness of the phrasing' in Pound's early poem 'The Garden':

> Like a skein of loose silk blown against a wall
> She walks by the railing of a path in Kensington
>   Gardens

As he put it, 'nobody that I knew of could have written more cleanly than that'. He was also fascinated by these lines from 'Canto II':

> Lithe turning of water,
>   sinews of Poseidon,
> Black azure and hyaline,
>   glass wave over Tyro.

The 'sense of cleanliness in the phrasing', the precision of the images, the ability to give the sea-god Poseidon a sculptural sense of presence with the word 'sinews' all contributed to this fascination. Tomlinson became immersed in American poetry: his tutor Donald Davie introduced him to the work of the American poets Wallace Stevens and William Carlos Williams. Davie became Professor of English at Essex University, a faculty which focused on the study of American influences on modern English poetry. Davie wrote the introduction to Tomlinson's poems, *The Necklace* (1955) which included the lines about space being made articulate (see Introduction, page 7). In the late 1950s and early 1960s Tomlinson visited America and met the poets Marianne Moore, William Carlos Williams, George Oppen and Louis Zukofsky.

The power of Pound's influence can be still be felt and his didactic voice offering advice to young poets still rings true:

> Use no superfluous word, no adjective which does not reveal something.
> Don't use such an expression as 'dim lands *of peace*'. It dulls the image. It mixes an abstraction with the concrete. It comes from the writer's not realising that the natural object is always the adequate symbol.

> ('A retrospect' in *Pavannes and Divisions*, 1918)

The Objectivists

This concentration upon the importance of individual objects led to the American poets, Williams, Oppen, Charles Reznikoff and Louis Zukofsky taking the name Objectivists. A renewed interest in Objectivist poetry has informed British poetry from the 1960s onwards. The Objectivists seemed to represent a radical movement in contemporary British poetry. However, Andrew McAllister, editor of the anthology *The Objectivists,* had also been the judge for the mainstream National Poetry Competition in 1995. This suggests perhaps that an interest in Objectivism didn't automatically separate one from the mainstream of poetry writing.

The principles informing their writing involved:

- fresh vocabulary

- musical shaping

- concentration on spare, radiant language.

The Objectivists produced ambitious lyric poetry sharpened by the experience of life in the fast-growing world of the big cities. Tomlinson, who came to know Oppen well in the 1960s and beyond, highlighted this importance of objects, things, in his poem 'In Memory of George Oppen'. In this poem Tomlinson contrasts the death in July 1966 of the New York poet Frank O'Hara in a motor accident at a party celebrating his fortieth birthday, with the slow decline of Oppen in his last years as a victim of Alzheimer's disease:

> We were talking of O'Hara.
> 'Difficult', you said
> 'to imagine a good death—*he died*
> *quietly in bed*, in place of:
> *he was run down*
> *by a drunk*.' And now, your own.
> First, the long unskeining year by year
> of memory and mind. You 'seemed
> to be happy' is all I hear.
> A lost self does not hide:
> what seemed happy was not you
> who died before you died. And yet
> out of nonentity, where did the words
> spring from when
> towards the end you told
> your sister, 'I don't know
> if you have anything to say
> but let's take out all the adjectives
> and we'll find out'—the way,
> lucidly unceremonious,
> you spoke to her in life and us.

We can hear those echoes from Pound's early advice to remove all superfluous adjectives still resounding – let objects, things, speak for themselves. Tomlinson's use of the word 'lucid' brings to the fore the idea of light: objects glowing with their own importance. At this point it is worth looking again at those two lines of Reznikoff's which so delighted Oppen (see page 18):

> Among the heaps of brick and plaster lies
> A girder, still itself among the rubbish.

The existence of the girder is highlighted by the busy-ness of the words surrounding it. With the opening seven words there is a feeling of the accumulation of rubbish and the sound of the last three words seals off the image at the centre: 'lies / A girder, still itself' with its further definition teased by the pun on the word 'still'. The importance of this way of looking at objects prompted Oppen to use a quotation from the 20th-century French philosopher, Jacques Maritain, as an epigraph to his 1962 volume of poems, *The Materials*:

> We awake in the same moment to ourselves and to things.

Thomas Hardy, Douglas Dunn and Ted Hughes

In 1973 the poet and critic Donald Davie published *Thomas Hardy and British Poetry*, a controversial book which asserted that 'the most far-reaching influence [on contemporary poets], for good and ill, has been not Yeats, still less Eliot or Pound, not Lawrence, but Hardy'. Davie suggests that any poet who is influenced by Thomas Hardy, the Wessex poet, is locked into a 'world of specific places at specific times'.

Hardy's most moving lyrics of loss, written soon after the death of his wife Emma in the winter of 1912, are placed in a particular time and in a particular local landscape, in contrast with the contexts chosen by Pound or Eliot. Eliot juxtaposed personal loss with 'fragments' from Western civilisation and Pound used far-reaching references to Greek mythology and Chinese history. Hardy's poetry, in contrast, occupies the walks and gardens, the rides and meadows which had provided the background to his courtship of Emma Lavinia Gifford in North Cornwall in 1870, as these verses from 'The Voice' show:

> Can it be you that I hear? Let me view you, then,
> Standing as when I drew near to the town
> Where you would wait for me: yes, as I knew you then,
> Even to the original air-blue gown!
>
> Or is it only the breeze, in its listlessness
> Travelling across the wet mead to me here,
> You being ever dissolved to wan wistlessness,
> Heard no more again far or near?

Donald Davie takes it for granted that Hardy had been the determining influence on Philip Larkin. He felt that Larkin had inherited 'lowered sights and patiently diminished expectations' from Hardy and from poems such as 'Hap', which refers to joy lying slain and accidents of chance which interrupt the flow of life:

> How arrives it joy lies slain,
> And why unblooms the best hope ever sown?
> – Crass Casualty obstructs the sun and rain.

Tone of voice

Hardy's series of moving elegies prompted by the death of his wife, Emma, caught an authentically convincing tone of grief in such pieces as 'The Going', 'The Voice' or 'After a Journey'. Donald Davie's thesis that Hardy is one of the founders of modern poetry is exemplified in Douglas Dunn's *Elegies*. Written after the death of Dunn's wife, Lesley, in March 1981, *Elegies* reveals the same haunting sense of presence-in-absence which runs through Hardy's verse. Dunn, a Scottish writer, had studied and worked at Hull University where Philip Larkin was the university librarian. In 'Home Again' Dunn refers to the look of his room in Hull as he returns to it after an absence of six weeks:

> The room is an aghast mouth. Its kiss is cold.
> I think of a piano with its lid locked
> And a carved, ivory silence in it.
> I look at a vase. It is too much to bear,
> For it speaks of a deranged expiry,
> An accusation of browned leafage.
> I see the falling off of its petals
> In a flashback of flowers, the white zig-zags,
> A snowfall of botanic ecstasy.
> A spirit shivers in the appled air,
> And I know whose it is.

There is an echo here of Hardy's 'The Walk', where he returns to be confronted by the difference made by his wife's death:

> What difference, then?
> Only that underlying sense
> Of the look of a room on returning thence.

Similarly, the presence of Hardy can be felt behind Ted Hughes's *Birthday Letters*, the sequence of poems addressed to his wife Sylvia Plath who had committed suicide in 1963. 'Visit' (see Part 3, page 81) contains these lines of raw grief:

> Just as when your daughter, years ago now,
> Drifting in, gazing up into my face,
> Mystified,
> Where I worked alone
> In the silent house, asked, suddenly:
> 'Daddy, where's Mummy?'

In terms of the undeniable seriousness of this inheritance from Hardy's lyrics, it is worth looking at what Peter Robinson says about poems addressing 'lived experience in recognisable forms of human expression':

> You've put your finger on something that absolutely baffles me about the contemporary poetry scene. I thought this was what poetry did or does, and it often doesn't seem to, strangely enough, because most poetry now isn't much like this.
>
> (Interview number six with Jane Davies in *Talk about Poetry*, 2007)

When the interviewer asked why this should be, Robinson replied that he was very puzzled by the way jokes are so important; he recounted how the Italian poet Franco Fortini had approached him at a poetry festival in Cambridge to ask 'Why do all the English poems end with a little laugh?' It seems almost as if an ironic tone is adopted in order to protect the poet from being seen as nakedly serious and wanting to refer to genuinely felt emotions.

The concluding words to Donald Davie's book are revealing in what they say about the differences between British and American poetry in the modern age:

> One is tempted to say that for many years now British poetry and American poetry haven't been on speaking terms. But the truth is rather that they haven't been on hearing terms – the American reader can't hear the British poet, neither his rhythms nor his tone of voice, and the British reader only pretends to hear the rhythms and the tone of American poetry since William Carlos Williams.

This conflict helped set the scene for the resurgence in British poetry.

Poetry wars and the British Poetry Revival

Peter Barry's account of the extraordinary situation in the 1970s when the Poetry Society was in effect hijacked is told in impressive detail in *Poetry Wars, British Poetry of the 1970s and the Battle of Earls Court*. The Poetry Society was founded in 1909 and was based in a Georgian terraced house in Earls Court Square, London. Barry suggests that the Society was 'the hub of a somewhat isolated poetry world, typified by the verse speaking competitions which were then its major source of income'. However, its journal, *Poetry Review*, became the most startling poetry magazine in the country while it was being edited by Eric Mottram from 1971 to 1977. According to Peter Barry, Mottram had suggested that the Poetry Society was 'the representative organisation for the amateur poetry lovers and weekend-poets who had never really recovered from the shock of the new, as exemplified by T.S. Eliot'. It represented many of those who hoped that the world of Eliot and Pound would simply die away and that one day modernism might yield the ground again to *Palgrave's Golden Treasury*, the anthology for poetry lovers first published by Francis Palgrave in 1861.

In his introduction to his account of the clash between modernism and traditionalists, Barry suggests that the radical poets of the 1960s and 1970s in England looked across the Atlantic for their role models. He highlights the enormously influential anthology *The New American Poetry 1945–1960*. This anthology contained work by the Black Mountain College poets (Charles Olson, Robert Creeley, Edward Dorn), the Beats (Allen Ginsberg, Gregory Corso and Gary Snyder) and the New York Poets (Frank O'Hara, John Ashberg and James Schuyler). As Barry puts it:

By the 1970s, a major resurgence of British poetry was taking place among poets who looked to these various 'dissenting' American poets for inspiration and example when the British scene seemed moribund.

In 1974 Eric Mottram christened this movement the British Poetry Revival and promoted the work of the new British poets in *Poetry Review,* which he edited. But by 1977 the 'establishment' had fought back and Mottram's contract as editor of the magazine expired. In fact, the poetry wars merely went underground and their impact was felt everywhere. Looking back over the six years of his editorship of *Poetry Review*, Mottram highlighted what he had felt to be important about the publication of new and challenging poetry:

> In *Poetry Review* anyone concerned with literature as a major function in society could find serious work; it was not a review for those who consumed poetry from time to time as a leisure pastime.
>
> (*Poetry Information*, 1979–1980)

The critic and novelist Raymond Williams said that the conflict within the Poetry Society was a head-on collision between poetry's residual and emergent worlds. Peter Barry suggests that it was a key moment in the history of contemporary British poetry, polarising the rift between the 'neo-modernists' who sought to continue the 1960s revival of the early 20th-century's modernist revolution, and the 'neo-conservatives' who sought to further the anti-modernist counter-revolution of the 1950s, best exemplified in the work and attitudes of Philip Larkin.

The differences between the world of the more established or traditional (mainstream) poetry written in the second half of the 20th century and the world of the British Poetry Revival are clearly highlighted by comparing the contents of the anthologies which have appeared over the past twenty-five years. The titles alone indicate some of the differences:

Mainstream

- *The Penguin Book of Contemporary British Poetry* (1982)

- *The New Poetry* (1993)

- *New British Poetry* (2004)

Modernist or British Poetry Revival

- *A Various Art* (1987)

- *Conductors of Chaos* (1996)

- *Other British and Irish Poetry since 1970* (1999)

- *Vanishing Points* (2004)

In terms of official recognition of the more challenging new styles of poetry being written in the second half of the 20th century, it is also important to look at the range of poets included by Keith Tuma in his authoritative *Anthology of Twentieth-Century British and Irish Poetry* (2001).

Closed / fixed form versus open form

One of the most important distinctions between traditional poetry and poetry of the British Poetry Revival is to do with form: the difference between **closed** or **fixed form** poems and **open form**.

- A closed form poem tends to adhere to a pattern which is readily identifiable in terms of its lines, metre and stanzas: for instance a sonnet has fourteen lines and a limerick has five. There may well be a consistent use of rhyme at the end of each line and the conclusion of the poem may yield a meaning, an answer to what the preceding lines have been building up.

- Open form poems possess a more organic structure which does not rely upon a development of regular patterns and these poems may well develop according to their own inner logic directed by an emotional impetus. An open form poem may have its structure dictated by the nature of its subject and may include collage-like references that do not automatically seem to follow each other in terms of consecutive appropriateness.

In the introduction to *Other: British and Irish Poetry since 1970*, Caddel and Quartermain associate a closed form of poetry with traditionalism. They list a narrow range of contemporary poets including Philip Larkin, Craig Raine and Simon Armitage. For Caddell and Quartermain:

> A typical poem is a closed, monolineal utterance, demanding little of the reader but passive consumption. Such a cultural vision has obviously been privileged not simply by the major publishing houses, but also by their attendant infrastructures of reviewing journals, 'literaries' and other elements of the media. The 'mainstream' is, for most of the United Kingdom population, for most of the time, the only perceptible stream.

Caddel and Quartermain's introduction to their anthology is a central document which deals with contemporary poetic issues (see Part 4, page 110). Having suggested that 'the British Isles have long been, self-evidently, crowded, complex, and packed with chaotic overlays of cultures – local, imported or created – which develop and intermix constantly', Caddel and Quartermain continue:

> Diverse cultures sometimes conflict violently, or sometimes make uneasy alliances, and sometimes, perhaps by chance, give rise to

the creation of new forms or achievements. About the only thing which is not possible in such a pluralistic, fragmenting, evolving society is a unitary, closed-system approach to culture, an insistence on a single 'great tradition' which can justify any degree of cultural domination. And yet at present the organs of this culture – from opera and literature to government – remain unshakably monolithic and centralised: to look at the central products of this culture is to be reminded just how assertive the 'mainstream' has been, and how marginalised its alternatives have seemed at times.

These comments are worth comparing with Don Paterson's introduction to his anthology *New British Poetry*:

The majority of the poetry actually read in the UK tends, quite simply, to demonstrate an allegiance to more traditional ideas of form and poetic closure than its more freewheeling, loose-lines, and open-ended North American equivalent – and perhaps also to the pure lyric, in the simplest and neutral sense of an abiding interest in the old song-forms.

Don Paterson also suggests that some catastrophic teaching of poetry in schools has led to the failure to develop a new generation of young readers. He refers to critical analysis of poems being dominated by an obsession with 'meaning' and reaffirms for us the need to be less **reductive** in our reading, so that we do not always try to reduce a poem to a simple phrase such as 'What does it mean?' After all, 'meaning' is not something that the clever poet has deliberately obscured so that the reader can follow the clues in order to de-code it (see Part 4 'Critical approaches', page 105). However, despite what Paterson says about 'meaning', his own anthology is unashamedly 'mainstream' and he uses that image of a river defiantly to reclaim its importance from those who attack it for being too traditional. He defines the 'mainstream' as 'a river with tributaries', allowing for other styles of poetry to be included. He continues the metaphor of the river to suggest that this 'mainstream' is 'a fairly furious and articulate torrent'. In supporting this view, his selection of poets for the anthology has been drawn from those who still sell books to a general readership rather than those who are only read by an academic public or by other poets.

Paterson makes it clear that he does not want to deny the importance of those other readerships. However, poetry which has lost its general audience will suffer from being seen as increasingly elitist, only to be read by the few, and almost taking a pride in not being understood. He continues:

For this reason, British poetry is occasionally described as 'populist'. This tends to mean no more than that it actively seeks an audience, often uses traditional forms, and considers itself primarily a kind of public art (with all the obligations to 'entertain', in the widest sense, that implies, whatever private meditations or epiphanies lie behind it). Popular, though, it isn't. By the standard of almost all other forms of literature, our sales are poor – perhaps a couple of thousand or a few hundred per book. Compared with the novel, poetry tends to enjoy very little in the way of support from publicity and marketing departments, bookstore reps, and the booksellers themselves; when these books do sell, they tend to do so largely by recommendation in the press or by word of mouth. This pays the books, I think, a considerable compliment.

Charles Olson, syllables and space

In *Angel Exhaust* (see extract from interview, page 15), R.F. Langley talked about the importance of reading the American Black Mountain poet, Charles Olson:

> I didn't start writing until I found out about American poetry. There was Donald Davie at Cambridge who talked about Pound. But Davie never talked about Olson. It was really Olson who convinced me that I might write something myself.

Langley commented upon the respect he felt for Olson's description of 'the dance of little syllables' in his seminal essay on *Projective Verse* (see extract in Part 3, page 95). In his essay, Olson suggested that the syllable was 'the king and pin of versification' that 'rules and holds together the lines, the larger forms, of a poem':

> It is by their syllables that words juxtapose in beauty, by these particles of sound as clearly as by the sense of the words which they compose.

> (*Charles Olson Reader*, 2005)

Ruth Padel prefaces comments about the syllable with the word's derivation from the Greek *sullambano* (from *sun*, 'with' and *lambano*, 'I grab hold'):

> A syllable is held together by letters, but it also makes active relationships with other syllables to form words. And in a poem it reaches out to and echoes syllables in other words to suggest connections and meanings.

> (*The Poem and the Journey*, 2007)

The idea of the syllable making active relationships with those which go before and after it takes up the point made in the Introduction about giving space a voice (see page 7). *Call Me Ishmael*, Olson's short study of Herman Melville's great American novel *Moby Dick*, opens with the words 'I take SPACE to be the central fact to man born in America'.

Olson was to become celebrated for heralding a type of poetry writing called 'Composition by Field', where the poet digs deep into the history and geography of a particular area. For instance, his major work, *The Maximus Poems*, takes the fishing-port of Gloucester, Massachusetts, as its base: early editions of the work had a map of the town on the cover. It is the nature of maps to be drawn to a consistent scale and they seem to suggest neutrality in that they don't represent a single viewpoint in the same way that an imaginative picture or a photograph might. 'Composition by Field' or 'Open Field' poetry, on the other hand, explores the world of different viewpoints, competing discourses, fragmented perceptions and memories. It becomes a type of collage which goes beyond offering the single viewpoint of an observer.

Olson was a leading figure at the North Carolina Black Mountain College which grouped together young poets and artists during the 1950s. His theories of poetry were introduced to England in the 1960s by Edward Dorn in *The North Atlantic Turbine*, the cover of which shows a map charting the Atlantic Ocean in terms of both geography and history. The lasting importance of the Black Mountain school of poetry was clearly emphasised in volume 12 of *The Oxford English Literary History 1960–2000* in which Randall Stevenson suggested that the

> Black Mountainous principles offered a complete escape from the formal restraints of Movement writing: a thoroughgoing alternative to its empirical conviction that significance could be readily derived from an observed world, and a stable identity assumed for the observer.

During the 1950s, The Movement group of poets were essentially English in character and were defined by their reactions against any Romantic ideas, concentrating instead upon rational and formal composition.

English poets who were influenced by the American Black Mountain world include Andrew Crozier, Lee Harwood and J.H. Prynne. Roy Fisher, another poet whose work from the 1960s onwards recognised the importance of the American influence, suggested that:

> The impact of the ideas current and made identifiable in that period was powerful and liberating and many of them still seem to me essential. There will have been a number of us, unknown to one another and widely dispersed, who found they had been living inside an imagined egg that was suddenly shattered.
>
> (*Starting at Zero*, published after an exhibition of Black Mountain College work, Arnolfini Gallery, Bristol, 2006)

The critic Peter Makin comments on two of Roy Fisher's later poems ('They Come Home' and 'Going', reprinted in full in Part 3, pages 93–94):

> To know where you are is to know your relation to this, and that, and something else; and that must mean to know the relation of those things to each other; ultimately, to acquire an ability to work towards predicting the location of everything in relation to your own, given the time and effort of correlation. The time and effort is what we pay the publishers of Road Atlases for, and also the astronomers, who are busy trying to sort out the new signals that emanate (with troubling frequency) from Ur-space and to relate them to the disturbed patterns of the old.
>
> (*Shearsman* 69 & 70, Autumn 2006 / Winter 2007)

Continuing her comments about syllables, Padel quotes the pianist Daniel Barenboim who said that music includes an awareness of how expression comes from the relationships of individual notes. Musical expression 'comes from linkage' and so when five notes are played each is in relation to the preceding note and the note that comes after. This is, of course, similar to the way individual syllables also work. When Peter Robinson was asked by Katy Price in the eighth of his 'Conversations' about how 'form' in poetry can 'take on meanings' he referred to space:

> Nowadays, I believe that poems themselves thematise the formal devices that shape them. After all, a caesura or an enjambment or a stanza-break are literally nothing. They are silence; they are white space. However, the words we use for them – a cut, a leap, a room-divide, are already all metaphorical. A silence can be made to signify almost anything, depending on what's around it.

Carol Rumens observed:

> It's easy to forget the obvious, that the spaces between the words are un-sounded. Unless a metrical expectation has been established … any desired caesura must be deliberately created, by punctuation or additional spacing. Otherwise, separate signifiers run into a single unit of melody until the end of the line.
>
> (*Self into Song*, 2007)

Finally, Simon Armitage wrote about space and the removal of the single observer's viewpoint in the introduction to his translation of *Sir Gawain and the Green Knight*, the long narrative poem written by an unknown author about the same time that Geoffrey Chaucer was writing *The Canterbury Tales*. He wrote:

The person who has become known as the Gawain poet remains as shadowy as the pages themselves. Among many other reasons, it is partly this anonymity which has made the poem so attractive to latter-day translators. The lack of authorship seems to serve as an invitation, opening up a space within the poem for a new writer to occupy.

(Introduction to *Sir Gawain and the Green Knight*, 2007)

▶ Can you see a connection between the different types of space discussed above by Padel, Olson, Robinson and Armitage?

Poetry publishing 1: poetry and the Internet

The world of small-press publication run by independent presses has been central to the growth of poetry over the last forty years and has enhanced the fertile interchange of American and English poetry from the 1960s onwards. For instance, Stuart Montgomery's Fulcrum Press had published Basil Bunting's *Briggflatts* in 1966 before going on to print volumes by Robert Duncan, George Oppen, Edward Dorn and Roy Fisher. John James's journal, *Resuscitator*, published Tomlinson alongside the New York Louis Zukofsky and MacSweeney and the Beat poet, Gary Snyder. Andrew Crozier ran Ferry Press and John Welch ran The Many Press, both based in London. One effect of this vibrant undercurrent of publication was that the big publishing houses did not 'own' the future of poetry reading in England. The invaluable work done in those years has, to a great extent, now been taken up by the world of Internet publishing.

The Argotist Online became the successor to the Liverpool University arts journal, *The Argotist*, which ran from 1996 to 2000. This online journal is devoted entirely to poetry and essays and contains a series of interviews with contemporary poets and publishers. The editor, Jeffrey Side, claims that it publishes 'non-mainstream poetry' and usefully defines this as 'poetry that is aware of the plasticity of language and which places connotation and ambiguity over denotation and precision of meaning'.

▶ Compare Jeffrey Side's definition of 'non-mainstream' with the comments (see page 26, above) about 'meaning' and 'closed' and 'open' forms of poetry. What are the benefits and dangers, when studying poetry, of using terms like 'mainstream' and 'non-mainstream' or 'closed' and 'open'?

Side suggests that non-mainstream poetry 'invites interpretation and allows for plurality of meaning as opposed to **hermeneutic** closure'. In one of the *Argotist* interviews, the poet Todd Swift was asked about the split between reading modernist or more traditional poetry. He replied that 'smart readers and poets read widely across the spectrum':

Poetry is language used in various ways. If you think language is for inquiry and exploration, you might not think it is about decorum and wit – hence the battle of Ancients and Moderns, which we are reliving now … Poetry doesn't evolve, but it does improve with time, and some of the innovative poets like Denise or Peter Riley will be read with pleasure in fifty years.

Poetry podcasts are now widely used and are not limited to the fringes: it is possible to hear the Poetry Society's National Poetry Competition winners, as well as interviews with the poets and contributions by the judges online. There has been an enormous increase in the amount of poetry and magazines about poetry published online. One of the most important is *Quid*, run by Andrea Brady and Keston Sutherland. *Quid* advertises itself as an occasional journal of poetics, criticism, invective and investigation. *Quid 13*, advertised as *IRA Quid*, contained poetic responses to the notorious atrocities committed by American soldiers at Abu-Ghraib prison in the aftermath of the 2003 Iraq war. Among these poems was 'Refuse Collection' by Jeremy Prynne, (see Part 3, page 100).

Litter, another online magazine, has been running since early 2005 and contains essays on visual arts, poetry reviews and poems. The magazine contains, amongst many other things, reviews of the work of Roy Fisher, Lee Harwood and Barry MacSweeney. Perhaps the most established magazine today is *Jacket*, run from Australia by John Tranter. Founded in 1997, it has included an interview with Roy Fisher and the publication of J.H. Prynne's 'Rich in Vitamin C', followed by an illuminating account of this poem given by John Kinsella, himself a poet and founder of *Salt Magazine*. (See Part 6, Resources, for web addresses.)

Poetry publishing 2: Shearsman, Salt and print-on-demand

Tony Frazer founded the poetry magazine *Shearsman* in 1981 and Shearsman Books was founded shortly after in 1982, in order to offer collections to authors involved with the magazine. The press converted to print-on-demand publishing for most titles in 2003. When asked in an interview for *The Argotist Online* about the world of digital printing, Frazer pointed out that a publisher's finances are less risky because

it is not necessary any longer to print 500 copies (or more) upfront and then hope that they will sell. The breakeven point for digital vs. traditional litho printing is about 500, litho being notoriously uneconomic for short-runs, but this assumes that the 500 litho-printed copies can be shifted in a fairly short time – which in most cases doesn't happen … It means that a publisher can take a risk on titles that (in other production methods) were too difficult to justify doing.

When asked about the effect of podcasting (including the various organisations that will take on anything without a set-up fee, simply sending royalties to an author), and whether poetry publishers still needed Arts Council subsidies, Frazer's reply reveals an important aspect of the world of the small publisher:

> Well, vanity publishers have always existed, and of course they've taken advantage of the new technology. Alas, having your book published by Xlibris, Lulu, PublishAmerica or Upfront isn't going to get you much attention or raise your profile. It might well give the amateur some satisfaction, but it's more or less self-publication. Regardless of the style of printing used, an imprint can develop a reputation, a brand name if you like. In 10 years Salt may well have dislodged Bloodaxe from pole position in UK sales. I wouldn't bet against it. The reason why 'publishers' have an advantage over 'packagers' is that there is an editorial process, and that is something that can be sold as a differentiator. A quality backlist adds to this. A lot of poets like to be published by Faber because of the aura cast by the shades of Eliot, Pound, Auden, Hughes, Heaney and Plath.

The independent publishing firm, Salt, which prints on demand, had its origins in 1990 when the poet John Kinsella launched his journal *Salt Magazine* in Western Australia. The journal rapidly developed an international reputation for publishing new poetry. In 2002 Kinsella joined Chris and Jen Hamilton-Emery to form a partnership which was soon publishing over forty books of poetry and literary criticism a year, earning an editor's award for excellence in literature in the 2006 American Book Awards. In 2006 they published *The Salt Companion to Peter Robinson*. It is the first full-length collection of essays devoted to Robinson's poetry and prose of thirty years, and provides a useful accompaniment to the *Talk about Poetry* interviews referred to earlier. The fourteen essays in *The Salt Companion* explore Robinson's poetic concerns: notions of place, personal and political responsibility, philosophy of language, music, painting and the art of the translator.

Poetry for the people

Small presses, poetry podcasts, poetry that is concerned with the philosophy of language and the art of the translator – all these things can make the poetry world of today sound either desperately narrow or desperately searching for a new audience. However, the poetry publisher Neil Astley reminds us of who we can be if we shake off academic elitism and celebrate voices both from our own communities and from around the world. Astley founded Bloodaxe Books in 1978, and is the editor of two bestselling poetry anthologies: *Staying Alive* and *Being Alive*. He suggests that:

> More people write poetry than go to football matches, and poetry is popular in schools, at festivals and at the hundreds of readings staged every week in pubs, theatres, arts centres and even people's homes. Poetry has reached a wider audience through films, radio, television and the internet, as well as through initiatives such as London's Poems on the Underground, which has been imitated around the world.
>
> ('Give Poetry Back to People', *New Statesman*, October 23, 2006)

In terms of the distinctions between so-called 'mainstream' and 'modernist' poetry Astley is quite scathing:

> Contemporary poetry has never been more varied, but what the public gets to hear about are the new post-Larkin 'mainstream' and the 'postmodern avant-gardists' (with their academic strongholds in Oxford and Cambridge respectively). More broad-based poetry expressing spiritual wisdom, emotional truth or social and political engagement is of little interest to either camp.

Astley also puts the emphasis firmly upon readers at a time when public interest in poetry seems to be growing rapidly. He sees the responsibility of the book publisher to heed a wake-up call before poetry publishing self-destructs:

> Internet sites are not enough. We need books.

▶ Contrast Neil Astley's comment about 'more broad-based poetry' with the comments by Jeffrey Side on 'mainstream ' and 'non-mainstream' poetry (page 31, above).

Poetry magazines

One reflection of this public interest in contemporary poetry can be seen in the number of poetry journals which are now available on the market. Often advertised on websites which contain selections of poems and articles, these journals are published in hard copy as well for subscribers. For example, Shearsman also produces its own poetry journal; in his *Argotist* interview Tony Frazer maintained that it is only possible to measure readership online up to a point (hits, visits and downloads), and the download may have been trashed within seconds. However, if someone buys a book or magazine then they are making a commitment that says more about the work:

I keep a print magazine going because a significant number of people seem to like the print version, and it's a good marketing tool for the main list of publications.

The most notable poetry journals at present are *PN Review*, *Tears in the Fence*, *Magma* and *The North*:

- From its inception in the 1970s *PN Review* has been dedicated to the principle that 'English poetry is a continuum in time and the practice as well as the reading of poetry benefit from a broad knowledge and understanding of the development of the art and craft'. Its contributors have included many of those who feature in this book including Heaney, Langley and Tomlinson.

- *Tears in the Fence* was started in 1984 by David Caddy. Alongside a wide range of contemporary poetry it published Barry MacSweeney's 'I Looked Down on a Child Today' and work by John Welch (see Part 3, pages 76 and 104).

- The editorial board of *Magma*, which has been running since the mid-1990s, look for poems which give a direct sense of what it is to live today – honest about feelings, alert about world, sometimes funny, always well-crafted. The title *Magma* is suggestive of the molten core of the world, hidden as deep feelings are and showing itself in unpredictable movements, tremors, lava flows, eruptions.

- *The North* was started in 1986 with Carol Ann Duffy as one of its earliest contributors. It also produces **chapbooks** of poetry, pamphlets and audio-cassettes under the Smith / Doorstep imprint.

Conductors of Chaos

The introduction to Iain Sinclair's controversial and combative anthology of modern poetry, *Conductors of Chaos*, sets down the battle lines between mainstream and other poetry in attractively uncompromising language:

> The work I value is that which seems most remote, alienated, fractured. I don't claim to 'understand' it but I like having it around. The darker it grows outside the window, the worse the noises from the island, the more closely do I attend to the mass of instant-printed pamphlets that pile up around my desk. The very titles are pure adrenalin: *Satyrs and Mephitic Angels*, *Tense Fodder*, *Hellhound Memos*, *Civic Crime*, *Alien Skies*, *Harpmesh Intermezzi*, *A Pocket History of the Soul*. You don't need to read them, just handle them: feel the sticky heat creep up through your fingers. If these things are 'difficult', they have earned that right. Why should they be easy? Why should they not reflect some measure of the complexity of the

climate in which they exist? Why should we not be prepared to make an effort, to break sweat, in hope of high return? There's no key, no Masonic password; take the sequences gently, a line at a time. Treat the page as a block, sound it for submerged sonar effects. Suspend conditioned reflexes … If it comes too sweetly, somebody is trying to sell you something.

Sinclair had been the series editor for the three short-lived 'Re/Active Anthologies' in the 1990s, the third of which contained work by Barry MacSweeney, Thomas A. Clark and Chris Torrance. Titled *The Tempers of Hazard* it was launched at the Compendium Bookshop in Camden High Street, London, but was rapidly pulped. As Sinclair was to put it in *Lights Out for the Territory,* referring to the media mogul who owned *The Sun* and *The Times* newspapers as well as Paladin Books:

Rupert Murdoch's accountants saw no reason to tolerate low-turnover cultural loss leaders.

In the late 1980s and early 1990s, Paladin Poetry published selections from the work of Andrew Crozier, Lee Harwood and Douglas Oliver. They also produced two outstanding anthologies of contemporary poetry, *The New British Poetry 1968–88* and *A Various Art* in 1990.

Rupert Loydell, editor of *Stride* magazine and founder of a publishing firm, interviewed Iain Sinclair and asked him about his combative introduction to *Conductors of Chaos*. Sinclair's response was to assert that the battle of the traditionalists and the moderns still continues:

The introduction was strategic, designed to infuriate the deadbeat verse-police who operate in the corners of broadsheets …

Loydell went on to suggest that print-on-demand publishers like Salt and Shearsman have continued the work started by Sinclair's Paladin anthologies and helped to create a new map of British poetry of the second half of the 20th century. Sinclair's response to Loydell, however, remained rather dismissive of any serious move forward in this respect and expressed a clear distrust of the New Labour image. He refused to accept that the publications of these new firms 'impacts on the flabby centre of things' and suspected that 'compulsory amnesia, the fog of spite, vanity and self-preservation' will never allow the challenging new world of a British Poetry Revival to replace conformity:

We have, after all, the most successful Poet Laureate [Andrew Motion] there has ever been, a customised New Labour figure: visible, camera-friendly, on the move – and positioned as far as it is possible to be from the heart of the matter, the old heat.

When questioned whether poetry has always been of minority interest, Sinclair replied:

> Poetry is intense. It takes time, concentration, intelligence: qualities that are not readily available. The payback is not instant. Populism is something else – and frequently involved with performance, staying on the road, like those Archie Rice vampire-figures who have been doing the festivals since the Second War (when the major schism occurred: the mask of English irony muzzled continental and transatlantic influences). This was mostly fear and careerism, but it worked.

Loydell then asked about the future of poetry publishing, 'the fantastic opportunity that is the possibilities of cheap production and dissemination of writing and music. Do you think print-on-demand publishing and the Internet will finally be accepted and change mainstream publishing?' Sinclair's reply highlighted the power of celebrity and gave a picture of the past twenty years: the media display of both politics and writing, Tony Blair's new-style advertising campaign for Britain in the 1990s ('Cool Britannia'), and the enormous success of Harry Potter.

> Look good, look wild-but-safe. Have a story. The author is being sold as much as the property. The answer is, as always, to ignore the system and stake out your own turf. Through Internet publishing, events, private circulation. Don't accept the fruit-fly demands of the chains: books don't lose value because they fail to shift thousands of units in the first week. It's bleak, but it always was. Time and place contrive the voices that time and place require.

▶ Do you think we will now see the likes of Tom Raworth, Allen Fisher and Lee Harwood take their rightful places in a poetic / literary canon alongside David Jones, Basil Bunting and W.S. Graham? Or is the postmodern world so fractured that any kind of critical agreement is no longer possible, or perhaps even desirable?

Poetry and politics

The political world of 1990s Britain: from Conservative to Labour

John Major's Conservative government which came into power in November 1990 after Margaret Thatcher's fall from power, is often seen as being limited and old-fashioned. His biographer, Anthony Selden, points to the nostalgic aura which surrounded his belief in traditional values: Major was mocked as a sentimentalist trying to bring back a rural lost England of the 1950s: an England of 'long shadows on county grounds, warm beer, invincible green suburbs, dog lovers and pool fillers and – as George Orwell once said – old maids bicycling to Holy Communion through the morning mist'. Whereas Margaret Thatcher's purpose had been to encourage an acquisitive and possessive individualism, giving strength to the voice of the consumer, Major insisted in his speech to the 1993 party conference that it was a time to return to those core values of neighbourliness, decency, courtesy, self-discipline and respect for the law, consideration for others. This perception of an old-fashioned world, ridiculed by cartoonists portraying Major as wearing his underpants outside his suit, seemed out of place in the decade leading up to the millennium. His belief in civilised behaviour and respect – a conservatism that 'came from what I saw, what I felt and what I did, as well as what I read' – was clearly expressed in his autobiography:

> It shaped what I wanted to do in office. When I was young my family had depended on the public services. I have never forgotten—and never will—what the National Health Service meant to my parents or the security it gave despite all the harsh blows that life dealt them.

His picture of England was unveiled to the public in his speech on 23 March 1991 when he coined the term 'Citizen's Charter', placing the emphasis firmly on the rights on the individual. One of the dangers of conservative nostalgic values has been highlighted by Andrew Duncan:

> Excessive love for the past leaves less psychological space for thinking about the future; at the worst, this makes you become a scholar, forking over the creativity of the past, and abandoning and suppressing your own creativity.

(*The Failure of Conservatism in Modern British Poetry*, 2003)

During the early 1990s, the Labour Opposition realised that it had to sever its links with a traditional past if it was to replace what was perceived as Conservative greyness; and in a world of 'Cool Britannia' and pop groups such as Stone Roses, Blur and Oasis the path was set for the promotion of Tony Blair, 'a regular sort of guy'. Blair's charisma and political dynamism were supported by his image as a young family man whose appeal seemed to be a shared normality. As the ideology of East European communism went through a meltdown, the emphasis now was on pragmatism: what mattered was what worked, the term 'the Third Way' was perfect for a post-ideological age.

'Blair's Babes' and 'The people's princess'

In the 1997 British general election, one hundred and twenty women MPs were elected to parliament (double the number from 1992) and there was a hope that feminist perspectives would be perceived more clearly and that women would have a more prominent role as legislative leaders. The photograph of ninety-six of them surrounding Tony Blair at Westminster, took on iconic status as an emblem of the new democracy, there were high hopes that there would be modernising changes in the style of government. The one hundred and one new women Labour MPs, however, were soon dubbed 'Blair's Babes' or 'back-wenchers' by the tabloid press and the misogynist tag became synonymous with passive support for the male-dominated Cabinet. It is worth here looking at Carol Ann Duffy's use of the word 'babe' in 'Little Red-Cap' (see Part 3, page 66) to register a feminist viewpoint towards stereotypical male behaviour. Although women's issues such as maternity pay, child care, part-time workers' rights, and a new deal for lone parents featured in the government's agenda, the reins of power remained firmly in male hands.

9/11

The attack on the World Trade Centre Twin Towers in New York on 11 September 2001, which killed nearly 4,000 people, was decisive in defining the 'War on Terror'. It led to coalition forces attacking Afghanistan, and the internment without trial at Guantanamo Bay of the first suspected terrorists. Six months after September 11, the American jurist, Richard Dworkin, warned that the greatest damage from the counterterrorist reaction had been to the long-cherished American legal defences of individual freedom. In March 2003, coalition forces from America and Britain invaded Iraq in the belief that Saddam Hussein possessed weapons of mass destruction. The shocking news which later came out of Iraq found a poetic response in Jeremy Prynne's 'Refuse Collection' (see Part 3, page 100). This poem has a brutally immediate impact which 'fuses a dizzying array of vocabularies, bringing into contact words and worlds that other writers would prise apart' (Colin Winborn, *PN Review 175*):

> To a light led sole in pit of, this by slap-up
> barter of an arm rest cap, on stirrup trade in
> crawled to many bodies, uncounted

The insultingly casual way the phrase 'slap-up' combines both violence and a party is juxtaposed with 'arm rest cap', suggesting relaxation. The image of 'cap' is then taken further in the poem where technology and decapitation are merged:

> Bite off the
> cap with a twist, upper strut invest cream off
> profit on a visor, bench law pressure why would
> you not credit that.

State of terror

The then British Home Secretary, Jack Straw, sparked controversy in 2001 by proposing to keep all fingerprints and DNA samples, even if a suspect was acquitted or never charged. This prompted strenuous protests from civil liberties groups who pointed out that the overwhelming majority of those stopped and searched were young black males; nevertheless, the Court of Appeal ruled that police could keep DNA and fingerprints from people charged but not convicted. The Criminal Justice Bill of 2005 enshrined this change.

Britain's involvement or compliance with the torture administered in Iraq prompted distrust. The extraordinary rendition flights in which the CIA transported terror suspects through British airports to deliver them for torture to places such as Jordan, Afghanistan and Saudi Arabia, where human rights seem not to possess the same value as in the West, raised an outcry and the Government was forced to admit in March 2006 that seventy-three such extraordinary renditions had occurred in the previous five years.

Foot and mouth disease

The 2001 outbreak of foot and mouth disease led to the culling of over six million animals; the spectacle of huge pyres of dead animals provided an unwelcome backdrop to the 2001 British election. Nicholas Johnson published his set of poems, *Cleave*, in 2002, as a memorial to the devastating crisis. The shocking sense of life being subsumed to large-scale economic demands is evident from the opening lines:

> February Monday a veiled dusk wet to the teeth
> over vast tumour fields where injection phials are set down.
> The herd gets its last meal, the straw's spread down,
> next, sedation. The culler goes in
> the bull taken out first.

A line from later in the poem, 'a pyre built so chronically it burnt ten weeks', reflects the photographs in the national press of cattle carcasses burning across Britain.

The radical power of poetry

In an account of contemporary British poetry which appeared in *Chicago Review* 2007, it was suggested that 'our identities, as we crouch over a laptop or eat a clementine on the subway, are dependent for their making and sustenance on the catastrophic exploitation of the unfortunate inhabitants of other places'. With a similar sense of urgency, the poet John Wilkinson wrote a piece for *Poetry Review* in summer 2003 where he looked closely at *Penniless Politics*, a book-length satirical poem by Douglas Oliver, and suggested that the energy and honesty of Oliver's work was far distant from the language of politicians:

I turned to a local station to watch a city hall debate about the expected invasion of Iraq, overwhelmingly hostile to the war. During an interlude, one of those venerable pundits in whom American TV delights, was asked why the country was on the brink of war: "Why? Why?" he choked – "Because out of the South West dust a fanatic, a *fanatic* with *Jesus* in his eyes came to send boys from the Bronx to die, and said to kids in Baghdad, on *their* birthdays it won't be candles on their cakes that get burnt, those kids will be set on fire and burnt by *our* missiles." His rage was so extreme and his age so advanced that I expected paramedics to rush into the studio. *Penniless Politic*s registers simultaneously both the outrageously obvious corruption of American democracy, and also this rude, demotic energy and honesty – the residual but still-visible radical power more often encapsulated and neutralised in official ideology.

It is in this context that the poetry being written today needs to be read.

Assignments

1   By researching and evaluating the publicity, reviews and websites for some of the anthologies mentioned, try to arrive at comprehensive and contrasting definitions of present-day mainstream and modernist poetry.

2   Compare a poem such as T.S. Eliot's 'The Love Song of J Alfred Prufrock' (1917) with a poem from one of the anthologies discussed. Can you see any ways in which Eliot's writing can be seen as an influence on the later poems?

3   Why are the poetry wars important?

4   Write a detailed review of two current poetry magazines, highlighting their particular features and discussing how narrow or wide a range of different types of poetry they promote.

5   Re-read the section 'Poetry and politics'. Do you think that any of the poems written about specific events (e.g. the First Iraq War, foot and mouth disease, etc.) are likely to make an impact once these events have faded into history?

6   Choose one of the quoted statements from either Ruth Padel or Peter Robinson, and use it as the starting point for an exploration of any poem in Part 3, Texts and extracts.

2 | Approaching the texts

- How important is 'meaning' in modern poetry?

- What are the central issues in women's poetry of the period?

- Could you describe war poetry of the period as being political in its aims?

- Has poetry in translation added another dimension to modern writing?

- What are the predominant features of Black poetry?

Mundane versus magic: comparisons to be made

In a newspaper article, Don Paterson emphasised the almost shamanistic or magical importance of the poet:

> Poetry is a dark art, a form of magic, because it tries to change the way we perceive the world. That is to say that it aims to make the texture of our perception malleable. It does so by surreptitious and devious means, by seeding and planting things in the memory and imagination of the reader with such force and insidious originality that they cannot be deprogrammed.
>
> (*The Guardian*, 6 November 2004)

He also made clear his belief in the skill, expertise and gift of the accomplished poet:

> Only plumbers can plumb, roofers roof and drummers drum; only poets can write poetry. Restoring the science of verse-making would restore our self-certainty in this matter; the main result of such an empowerment would be the rediscovery of our ambition, our risk, and our relevance, through the confidence to insist on the poem as possessing an intrinsic cultural value, of absolutely no use other than for its simple *reading*.

Rod Mengham shares some common ground with Don Paterson in his concern for the relationship between poets and their readers. However, he also highlights significant differences, where the world of 'understanding' is challenged by that of 'imagination'. The language used by Mengham is, interestingly, also more combative than that of Paterson:

> The vanishing point lies beyond the horizon established by ruling conventions, it is where the imagination takes over from the understanding. Most anthologies of contemporary verse are filled with poems that do not cross that dividing-line, but our contention

is that many poems in this volume are situated on the threshold
of conventional sense-making. They go beyond the perspective of
accepted canons of taste and judgement and ask questions about
where they belong, and who they are meant for, often combining the
pathos of estrangement with the irascibility of the refusenik.

(Introduction to *Vanishing Points*, 2004)

As a way of trying to tease out some of the differences between so-called 'meaning'
and what lies on the margins of meaning and imagination, it is interesting to look
at two poems which are intriguingly linked. The first is by the American poet, Frank
O'Hara, and the second by the English poet Simon Armitage.

O'Hara's 'A Step Away From Them' (one of his most famous poems) celebrates
both life and death. O'Hara's biographer, Brad Gooch, called it 'a record for history
of the sensations of a sensitive and sophisticated man in the middle of the 20th
century walking through what was considered by some the capital of the globe'. It
is one of O'Hara's so-called 'lunch poems', written after midday strolls through the
noisy and splintered glare of Manhattan. In August 1956, responding to the deaths
of Bunny Lang, a writer and eccentric whom he had known since Harvard, and the
painter Jackson Pollock whose fatal car crash happened some days before, O'Hara
wrote the first of what he was later to refer to as his 'I do this I do that' poems:

It's my lunch hour, so I go
for a walk among the hum-colored
cabs. First, down the sidewalk
where laborers feed their dirty
glistening torsos sandwiches
and Coca-Cola, with yellow helmets
on. They protect them from falling
bricks, I guess. Then onto the
avenue where skirts are flipping
above heels and blow up over
grates. The sun is hot, but the
cabs stir up the air. I look
at bargains in wristwatches. There
are cats playing in sawdust.

               On
to Times Square, where the sign
blows smoke over my head, and higher
the waterfall pours lightly. A
Negro stands in a doorway with a
toothpick, languorously agitating.
A blonde chorus girl clicks: he

smiles and rubs his chin. Everything
suddenly honks: it is 12:40 of
a Thursday.

        Neon in daylight is a
great pleasure, as Edwin Denby would
write, as are light bulbs in daylight.
I stop for a cheeseburger at JULIET'S
CORNER. Giulietta Masina, wife of
Frederico Fellini, è bell' attrice.
And chocolate malted. A lady in
foxes on such a day puts her poodle
in a cab.
        There are several Puerto
Ricans on the avenue today, which
makes it beautiful and warm. First
Bunny died, then John Latouche,
then Jackson Pollock. But is the
earth as full as life was full, of them?
And one has eaten and one walks,
past the magazines with nudes
and the posters for BULLFIGHT and
the Manhattan Storage Warehouse,
which they'll soon tear down. I
used to think they had the Armory
Show there.
        A glass of papaya juice
and back to work. My heart is in my
pocket, it is Poems by Pierre Reverdy.

The poem has a style which resembles a handheld camera as O'Hara heads on west during his lunch hour and then downtown from the museum, past construction sites on Sixth Avenue, through Times Square where he stops for a cheeseburger and a glass of papaya juice beneath the Chesterfield billboard with blowing smoke, and then back uptown to work.

This seizing on moments, the tiny objects, the enticing sights and sounds of the everyday bring to life an intensity of gaze, a celebration of the moment. However, as Marjorie Perloff comments,

for every exotic sight and delightful sensation, there are falling bricks, bullfights, blow outs, armories, mortuaries, and, as the name Juliet's Corner suggests, tombs …

(*Poetry On & Off the Page, Essays
for Emergent Occasions*, 1998)

The fragility of the everyday is caught melting between the Puerto Ricans who make the day 'beautiful and warm' and the end-of-line word 'First' which heralds the references to the death of three close friends. The poet here seems to be not only a step away from the dead but also from the fast movement of the day, as sensations disappear almost as soon as they are presented.

Simon Armitage's poem appears as the second of two which simply have the title 'Poem', published in *Penguin Modern Poets 5*. The first of the two poems opens with the lines:

> Frank O'Hara was open on the desk
> but I went straight for the directory.
> Nick was out, Joey was engaged, Jim was
> just making coffee and why didn't I
>
> come over.

These easy moving lines are a clear imitation of O'Hara's 'I do this I do that' style and the use of individual names give a personal informality to the tone. This is the second of the two poems.

> And if it snowed and snow covered the drive
> he took a spade and tossed it to one side.
> And always tucked his daughter up at night.
> And slippered her the one time that she lied.
>
> And every week he tipped up half his wage.
> And what he didn't spend each week he saved.
> And praised his wife for every meal she made.
> And once, for laughing, punched her in the face.
>
> And for his mum he hired a private nurse.
> And every Sunday taxied her to church.
> And he blubbed when she went from bad to worse.
> And twice he lifted ten quid from her purse.
>
> Here's how they rated him when they looked back:
> sometimes he did this, sometimes he did that.

This poem moves in a relaxed manner from event to event with the intention of giving a portrait of the central character. The repetition of 'And' which opens all but three lines of this sonnet gives the reader a sense of the accumulation of detail which will amount to the portrait. However, compared with the details of O'Hara's 'A Step Away From Them', they seem to be locked into banality. The portrait achieved gives the reader the impression that the man is little more than a sentimental accumulation of clichéd reactions: he 'tucked' his daughter up, conveying an image of warm parenthood and he reliably 'tipped up' his wages for the family – a dismissive tone reminiscent of emptying bins. He moves between praising his wife for cooking meals, an accepted form of gratitude, to punching her – where the addition of the words 'in her face' adds a grim feeling of thoughtless violence. Any emotion of grief at the death of the man's mother is reduced to platitude with the use of the word 'blubbed' and, as if to emphasise his ordinariness, it is followed by a reference to what is seen as a type of normality:

> And twice he lifted ten quid from her purse.

This is a clever poem where the word 'lifted' is juxtaposed with the 'tipped up' in reference to money earlier on. We are presented with a man whose life can be contained within the phrase 'sometimes he did this, sometimes he did that' with its clear reference to O'Hara's style of writing, but we are left with a sense of thinness. Where O'Hara has managed to move from the accumulation of particular details to a register of deep loss and a recognition of both the vulnerability of life and its fragility, Armitage's 'Poem' remains satisfied with its wit, its cleverness as pastiche.

▶ How much does the contrast between the open free-verse form of O'Hara's poem and the closed sonnet form adopted by Armitage influence your reaction to these two poems?

Interviewed in January 2002 by Mike Alexander, Armitage said that he thought that there had been more interest in 'form' in British poetry over the last ten or fifteen years than there had been in the period just preceding it. He went on to suggest that Britain might be categorised as a country which in some way experimented with and then rejected modernism:

> I think there's also something about a legacy, and the heritage of poetry within Britain, which has been one of speaking to a general rather than a specialised reader. Formal poetry, formal poems, tend to be more memorable, tend to be the ones that go down best – crudely speaking. I don't know whether it's specifically about using sonnets, but if you flip through a lot of books of contemporary British poetry, you will come across a lot of poems with fourteen lines in them.
>
> (Interview during San Miguel Poetry Week, 2002)

▶ As a further contrast with Armitage's poem and with his comments above, read Barry MacSweeney's poem 'I Looked Down on a Child Today' (Part 3, page 76).

MacSweeney's poem refers to a tragedy, witnessed by the poet, of a child killed by a bus in the centre of Newcastle-on-Tyne. It relies on an accumulation of detail for its effect. The repetition of 'I' focuses on the witness of the scene, but the young girl's death is placed against a historical and social background of the history of Gallowgate, 'where as a living they hanged / prisoners for bread-theft'. The girl's 'blind wonderful enthusiasm for life' is placed against a background of 'the strategy of the masses' whose needs are only addressed 'through the tills / where paper receipts come clicking out increasingly slowly to / everyone's annoyance'.

Modern women poets 1: dramatic monologues

> Thin beautifully etched ice – over such deep shocking water.

Ted Hughes's comment on the work of the poet Vicki Feaver may well be applicable to other women poets, such as Carol Ann Duffy who, like Feaver, use the genre of the **dramatic monologue.**

Dramatic monologues

A key issue behind much feminist poetry from the 1990s and beyond revolves around the extent to which the identity of a woman is moulded by the attitude of society to women in general. The dramatic monologue as a style of writing allows the poet to explore the complexities within a relationship.

> As a genre the dramatic poem, most particularly the monologue, works as a place in which the unstable selfhood of the female poet can comfortably reside, providing a position which problematises and at the same time explores issues of gender, and identity, as well, potentially as 'race', class, nation.
>
> (*Consorting with Angels, Essays on Modern Women Poets* by Deryn Rees-Jones, 2005)

This exploration of problems, and different, often conflicting ways of seeing things, is evident in Vicki Feaver's 'Judith' (see Part 3, page 65), based on an Old Testament story. Judith is in the tent of Holofernes with the express purpose of killing him, but she has conflicting feelings. Although her duty is to avenge her dead husband and to save her city from the rapacious onslaught of the Assyrian army, she feels 'a rush / of tenderness' when looking at Holofernes' sleeping body. She is sexually tempted by the sight of him and even sees herself in the stereotypical role of the lover who wishes 'to melt like a sweet on his tongue'. Judith is brought back from the brink of this immersion in the male's dominance by a recollection of her dying husband whose body is 'already cooling / and stiffening' as she reaches it across a stubble field. The 'cooling' carries to the reader the sense of the dissolving of her arousal by the body of Holofernes and the reference to 'stiffening' is more related to her resolve than a reflection of masculine sexuality. The lead-up to her beheading of the Assyrian leader is conveyed in terms of brutality and rape where her 'emptiness' is like 'the emptiness of a temple / with the doors kicked in'.

Vicki Feaver's own comments on the writing of this poem, quoted in Rees-Jones' book, are worth close scrutiny:

> I kept asking myself questions in my notebook and trying to answer them. 'How can a woman be capable of violence? How be the opposite of everything she'd been brought up to be? What is the motive? Rage? What rage? The rage of grief?' I tried to imagine Judith's state of mind, rather like an actress does to get into a part. ('She has to keep him believing that she's fallen in love with him, that she's going to let him sleep with her—she has to bring out his best instincts; and in that moment when she does, she almost falls in love with him' ... 'I think she must have come to love the man she was going to kill, or she could not have done it.') In the end I almost became Judith; though I was obviously ambivalent about this close personal identification because the early drafts of the poem veer between a first person voice and a safe, more distant, third person narration ... It is obvious to me now that the poem was a vehicle for the grief and rage I was feeling when I wrote it. The story is Judith's but the emotions are mine.

That last statement accounts perhaps for the appropriateness of dramatic monologues where the recovery of prominent and usually neglected figures from history offers a useful vehicle for writing about personal emotions, whilst at the same time preserving a sense of distance.

The dramatic monologue conveys in its very name a sense of the stage and, as with acting, it is possible to construct for ourselves an imaginary body out of which the voice of our inner feelings can be spoken. By openly 'acting' one can put a convenient and perhaps self-protective barrier between the expression of one's real feelings and an awareness of how unpopular these feelings might be to the audience. A collection of poems made up of dramatic monologues allows many different voices to be heard, as well as mischievously emphasising the artificiality which women may sense in the way their roles in life are constructed by men. Carol Ann Duffy's volume *The World's Wife*, for instance, takes a list of iconic historical and mythical characters and gives the wife's version. The tale of Eurydice traditionally has Orpheus, the poet and musician, going down to the Underworld to bring back to life his beloved wife; in Duffy's poem 'Eurydice' (1999), Eurydice does not want to be rescued. As she says, being dead 'suited me down to the ground': the place of 'Eternal Repose' was a welcome relief from being required to feed the vanity of her poet-husband:

who follows her round
writing poems,
hovers about
while she reads them,
calls her His Muse,
and once sulked for a night and a day
because she remarked on his weakness for abstract nouns.

Modern women poets 2: fairytale and myth

Like the use of dramatic monologue, an interest in myth and fairytale is a
recognisable attempt to remove the poet's self from a lyrical expression into an
embodied narrative. Traditional fairytales have a residual power of rethinking the
roles of women and the ways they are represented within society. In her essay,
'Myth and Fairytale in Contemporary Women's Fiction', Susan Sellars suggests that
the world of myth can reflect human feelings in a manner which is very different
from the day-to-day subject-matter of poems which are firmly based in a modern
urban environment:

> The communal process of telling and retelling a myth until it contains
> the input of many in a pared down form has the paradoxical effect of
> reflecting our experiences more powerfully than if we were to retain
> a profusion of personal details.
>
> (from *Consorting with Angels,* 2005)

For instance, in Duffy's version of Little Red Riding-Hood, 'Little Red-Cap' (see
Part 3, page 66), the reader is confronted with those recognisable traits of male
seduction which have become clichéd. The narrator – these poems, too, are
dramatic monologues – is exposed to 'the greying wolf' who 'howls the same old
song at the moon' – a vision of the ageing trendy who still uses the same old chat-
up lines. The girl could almost be a young version of Eurydice as she comes across
the wolf in the clearing 'reading his verse out loud / in his wolfy drawl'. The sadness
of a dream of romance turning into the mundane nature of conventional types is
caught splendidly in the lines:

> Then I slid from between his heavy matted paws
> and went in search of a living bird – white dove –
>
> which flew, straight, from my hands to his open mouth.

A gesture of peace and purity is converted into domestic consumption: the woman
provides her man with breakfast in bed! Some of Duffy's female narrators allow
the poet to indulge in outrageously vivid feelings of transgressing all rules. For
instance, Salome, in the poem of that title (1999), wakes up in bed in the morning

after a night out on the tiles to find a strange man next to her whose name she cannot even remember. Veering away from the myth of Herod's stepdaughter who danced provocatively so that she could demand in return the head of John the Baptist, this Salome has the man she has picked up last night lying next to her in bed:

> Never again!
> I needed to clean up my act,
> get fitter,
> cut out the booze and the fags and the sex.
> Yes. And as for the latter,
> it was time to turn out the blighter,
> the beater or biter,
> who'd come like a lamb to the slaughter
> to Salome's bed.
>
> In the mirror, I saw my eyes glitter.
> I flung back the sticky red sheets,
> and there, like I said—and ain't life a bitch—
> was his head on a platter.

▶ Compare 'Little Red-Cap', the opening poem in *The World's Wife*, with 'Demeter', which closes the book. ('Demeter' is included in full in Part 3 [see page 67] and it is analysed more fully in Part 5 [see page 114].)

In Duffy's poem 'Demeter', issues of loss and coming to terms with living a life without love are expressed through the mouth of the Greek mythological figure, Demeter. Demeter's daughter Persephone was ripped from her by Hades to spend part of the year in his kingdom of the underworld. In mythology Demeter became associated with the grieving world of winter as she waited for the return of her daughter, together with the spring flowers:

> Where I lived – winter and hard earth.
> I sat in my cold stone room
> choosing tough words, granite, flint,
>
> to break the ice.

Duffy's later volume *Rapture* explores ideas about the healing and restorative forces of love – see for example 'If I Was Dead' (Part 3, page 68). Duffy emphasised the underlying sense of acting or performance when she performed the work with a jazz background, and when some of the poems were sung by the musician Eliana Tomkins at the book's launch in 2005. Such an emphasis on dramatic performance seems deliberately to allow the performer to be less identified with the first person singular of the nakedly moving lyric voice.

The use of mythology can also enable personal experience to be transformed into a political statement. The role of the poet in relation to the character created can be seen clearly in 'The Handless Maiden' by Vicki Feaver:

When all the water had run from her mouth,
and I'd rubbed her arms and legs,
and chest and belly and back,
with clumps of dried moss;
and I'd put her to sleep in a nest of grass,
and spread her dripping clothes on a bush,
and held her again—her heat passing
into my breast and shoulder,
the breath I couldn't believe in
like a tickling feather on my neck,
I let myself cry. I cried for my hands
my father cut off; for the lumpy, itching scars
of my stumps; for the silver hands—
my husband gave me—that spun and wove
but had no feeling; and for my handless arms
that let my baby drop—unwinding
from the tight swaddling cloth
as I drank from the brimming river.
And I cried for my hands that sprouted
in the red-orange mud—the hands
that write this, grasping
her curled fists.

The distant story and the personal nature of the poet writing the poem are brought together in the last lines in a manner that recalls the earlier work of both Ted Hughes in 'The Thought-Fox' and Seamus Heaney in 'Digging'.

▶ Read these poems by Hughes and Heaney and 'The Handless Maiden'. Does the dramatic monologue form of Feaver's poem give it greater or less impact than the other two?

In a journal entry which she wrote about her creative processes, Feaver said:

I am the handless maiden, writing my story with my new grown hands ... the typewriter is a distraction. I want poems to come out of my own hand, my body.

Deryn Rees-Jones suggests that:

The hands which re-grow in Feaver's poem become an image of the powerless and wrongly-punished female who is regenerated in her resuscitation of her daughter with her curled fists. Hands in the poem become a specifically female symbol for Feaver, not simply because of their connection with the maternal, but because they come to represent something "natural" and "authentic" by way of juxtaposition with the silver man-made hands the Maiden's husband gives her (for which we might parallel Feaver's desire not to use a typewriter). Importantly, too, it is the bond of love between mother and daughter which sees the mother's damaged limbs restored, and this restoration occurs in another feminised space in the poem, the river's 'red-orange mud' that holds echoes of the red jelly or the menstrual blood that is threaded throughout the collection.

(*Consorting with Angels*, 2005)

Perhaps the last word should be left to Carol Rumens, whose own dramatic conversation appears in 'From a Conversation During Divorce' (see Part 3, page 69). In her poem Rumens has only one speaker, but from the nature of what she says we can visualise and hear the separated partner. For instance, when the poem opens with her assertion that she will 'go back one day', we can hear the mistaken reaction to her words by the way she is compelled to follow it up so quickly with 'Visit, that is.' The house which the speaker has abandoned seems cold to the partner left behind, and the size of its emptiness seems to grow with absence:

It used to be warm in the days
Before I decided to go,
And it didn't seem big at all,

In fact, it was rather small,
Which is partly the reason I...

After all, truths are comparative and it was the feeling of being confined in a small place which partly accounted for the move; it is helpful to take note of Rumens' comment in her lectures *Self into Song* referred to in Part 1 (see page 30):

Our most intimate connection with language is through poetry, because it allows such a dense interplay of verbal responses.

War

In his introduction to the anthology *100 Poets Against the War* (2003), Todd Swift points to the importance of W.H. Auden's poem 'September 1, 1939'. Auden's poem shows his bleak vision of the world, seen from New York as World War Two opens:

I sit in one of the dives
On Fifty-Second Street
Uncertain and afraid

As the clever hopes expire
Of a low dishonest decade:
Waves of anger and fear
Circulate over the bright
And darkened lands of the earth,
Obsessing our private lives;
The unmentionable odour of death
Offends the September night.

...

Into this neutral air
Where blind skyscrapers use
Their full height to proclaim
The strength of Collective Man,
Each language pours its vain
Competitive excuse:
But who can live for long
In an euphoric dream;
Out of the mirror they stare,
Imperialism's face
And the international wrong.

These last two lines go far beyond an individual war; this recognition of the universality of suffering and the consequences of warfare become highlighted with frightening immediacy in Tony Harrison's *A Cold Coming* (see Part 3, page 86). This poet's concern for making the reader recognise the complicity he must share with the horror he witnesses on television and in the newspapers is structurally central to Harrison's long poem. *A Cold Coming* was composed as an initial response to the photograph of the charred corpse of an Iraqi soldier sitting at the wheel of his burnt-out army truck on the road to Basra during the First Gulf War in 1991. The photograph was reproduced worldwide, including in the *Guardian*, which then commissioned Harrison to write the poem. It was also reproduced on the front cover of the first edition of *A Cold Coming*: like the missile in George Oppen's 'Time of the Missile' (see Part 1, page 17) it has an inescapable presence. *A Cold Coming* opens with a reference to three 'wise soldiers from Seattle' who take the precaution of banking their sperm (a pun on 'cold coming') so that they may have a sense that life continues beyond their own individual fate:

So if their fate was to be gassed
at least they thought their name would last,

and though cold corpses in Kuwait
they could by proxy procreate.

As with many of his poems, Harrison places the scene within a perspective of classical and literary reference. The three 'wise soldiers' are modern counterparts of the three wise men who went to celebrate a different birth two thousand years ago. A reference to Sophocles points to the Greek tragedian's philosophy that you can call no man happy until he has died. However, linked in with this witty and sardonic humour is a moment of genuine feeling which is movingly simple in its expression of human need. The charred Iraqi speaks, like one of the dead from Dante's *Inferno*:

> Though all Hell began to drop
> I never wanted life to stop.
>
> I was filled with such a yearning
> to stay in life as I was burning,
>
> such a longing to be beside
> my wife in bed before I died,
>
> and, most, to have engendered there
> a child untouched by war's despair.

Furthermore, there is a possible **intertextual** link to an anonymous English poem from the 15th century:

> Western wind when wilt thou blow
> The small rain down can rain –
> Christ, if my love were in my arms
> And I in my bed again.

The American poet Charles Olson included this short piece of highly charged verse in his essay 'Projective Verse' (see Part 3, page 95):

> It is by their syllables that words juxtapose in beauty, by these particles of sound as clearly as by the sense of the words which they compose. In any given instance, because there is a choice of words, the choice, if a man is in there, will be, spontaneously, the obedience of his ear to the syllables. The fineness, and the practice, lie here, at the minimum and source of speech.

The syllabic simplicity of the second line, 'The small rain down can rain', emphasises the mournful sense of loss felt by the poet. This is followed by the emphatic expletive 'Christ' at the opening of the third line, which captures that yearning for the return of a world now gone. This short poem is discussed further in Part 4 (see page 107).

The language used by Harrison throughout *A Cold Coming* is explicitly related to media coverage. The charred corpse speaks to the poet:

> Don't be afraid I've picked on you
> for this exclusive interview.

And the poet-reporter responds in appropriate manner by holding

> ...the shaking microphone
> closer to the crumbling bone

Since we live in a world of live 'reality' television shows and there is an interest in capturing images of disaster as they happen, this ironic stance by Harrison is particularly haunting and effective. The pictures of the planes crashing into the World Trade Centre on 9/11, 2001, the use of mobile phones as cameras, the capturing of the immediate which has been satirised amongst others by Oliver Stone in his 1994 film, 'Natural Born Killers', have all brought us closer to the world of events as they happen. On the Internet, social networking sites have been used to spread moving images of teenage fights recorded on mobile phones in parks, alleys and car parks.

W.H. Auden wrote about the inability of poetry to have a lasting effect on matters of life and death, and its powerlessness to prevent things happening:

> For poetry makes nothing happen: it survives
> In the valley of its saying where executives
> Would never want to tamper; it flows south
> From ranches of isolation and the busy griefs,
> Raw towns that we believe and die in; it survives,
> A way of happening, a mouth.
>
> ('In Memory of W.B. Yeats', 1939)

Perhaps that last statement about poetry's 'mouth' is one of the most powerful inspirations for those who register their protests against modern warfare. It clashes with the decision of the First Lady, Laura Bush, to host an apolitical poetry reading at The White House in 2003 when her husband was planning the invasion of Iraq. Todd Swift's account of his poetic response to this poetry reading illustrates the increasing power of the Internet in terms of poetry writing and publication to a wide audience:

> On January 19, 2003, Sam Hamill sent out an email, protesting against the First Lady's decision ... and on January 20, the author of this introduction invited poets world-wide to send antiwar poems to a modest London-based webzine (www.nthposition.com) – it is safe to say that neither of us expected the grass-roots surge of support we began to receive, almost immediately. In the case of the White

House peace protests, their web site has gone on to collect 10,000 poems from prize-winners to inspired amateurs; and Nthposition received over one thousand emails.

(Introduction to *100 Poets Against the War*, 2003)

The first electronic chapbook of anti-war poems was launched on the same day that Hans Blix's weapons' inspections report was delivered to the UN. (Hans Blix was the Chief Weapons Inspector sent by the United Nations to Iraq to find the 'weapons of mass destruction' that were the main pretext for invading Iraq; they were never discovered but Iraq was invaded nevertheless.) Swift's reaction to Auden's 'poetry makes nothing happen' may be seen in his answer given to interviewers, who asked if he thought that this instant publication of poems could prevent war from happening:

> My reply has been that I am not naive, and that I know that very few books in history have had such an effect on 'civilised' nations. Often just the opposite. It is fair to say, though, that poems express an attentive approach to language, experience, and human fragility, which can often show up the false linguistic contortions of the impresarios of spin, in office or war room. More importantly, such poems witness to the presence of opposition to illegal violence at a time when many in power would like to pretend to the moral high ground.

100 Poets Against the War contains a wide range of poetical reaction to the war against Iraq. Some poems, like 'The Man of Principle' by Mr Social Control, provocatively question the nature of definitions concerning who is a terrorist and who a freedom-fighter. If you wonder whose definition of a word is being used, it is worth bearing in mind Toni Morrison's sharply uncompromising statement in her anti-slavery novel, *Beloved*: 'definitions belonged to the definers – not the defined'.

> I absolutely refuse to go
> on this insane and murderous
> suicide bombing mission to Oxford Circus
> unless
> we first have the full agreement
> of the United Nations Security Council.

Other contributions to this remarkable anthology register a quiet, elegiac tone, reminding the reader of war's universality, such as 'A Natural History of Armed Conflict' by Pat Boran:

> The wood of the yew
> made the bow. And the arrow.
> And the grave-side shade.

The combination of personal and domestic response to war is movingly caught by the Bristol poet, Tony Lewis-Jones, in 'At Home, At War' (2003):

> Now there is silence in the house, except
> The pipes tap-tapping under floorboards and
> The clocks' slow rhythmic messages. You are
> Late coming home for an argument:
> The night holds terrors every parent knows.
> Your mother is away. She, I'm certain,
> Would have played this same weak hand
> Quite differently. The morning paper
> Demonstrates with images how words
> Can lose all meaning: mouths that cannot speak
> Tell how desperately we need to understand.
> Wars begin when language fails us. The missiles
> Fall, undiverted by the right command.

It is significant that some of the poets in the anthology were already public voices: the connection between poetry and the public face of the media is emphasised by the fact that Lewis-Jones had held the post of poet-in-residence at BBC Radio Bristol, 1997–1998; Mr Social Control is a London-based performance poet who had frequently been broadcast on BBC radio and who had released a live CD, *The War Against Abstract Nouns*, in 2002.

Answering a comment made in the *Times Literary Supplement* early in 2007 that no poet of distinction 'has borne down on the wars in Afghanistan and Iraq with the authority of direct experience', Jeremy Noel-Tod pointed out that the most recent publication by J.H. Prynne, 'To Pollen', was directly concerned with the war on terror and its vicious circles, especially in terms of the media's promotion of war as something to be looked at on screen – an ironic 'live' broadcasting:

> Natural-born killers, their white song camera is ours
> for the same, to feed a habit nurtured by wound drainage
> or yet waste out mortality.

▶ Compare 'September 1, 1939' with *A Cold Coming*. Is there a shared sense of anger which is recognisable despite there being 52 years between Auden's poem and Harrison's?

▶ Are there any other recognisable similarities between the two poems?

▶ What common ground can you find between Auden's comments upon language and the ideas expressed in both Lewis-Jones' poem and the so-called interview given by the dead Iraqi in Harrison's *A Cold Coming*?

Poetry in translation: Heaney and Hughes

Two of the giant figures of poetry shadowing the last forty years, Seamus Heaney and Ted Hughes, have both been closely involved in translating poetry into English and, in a sense, making it their own. T.S. Eliot's lecture, 'What Dante Means to Me' (referred to in Part 1, page 11), gives an account of the central importance of the 13th-century Florentine poet. Heaney had recognised the importance of Dante to Eliot in his own lecture, 'Learning from Eliot', delivered at Harvard in 1988:

> It is true, of course, that Eliot's pure mind was greatly formed by the contemplation of Dante, and Eliot's dream processes fed upon the phantasmagoria of *The Divine Comedy* constantly, so the matter of Dante's poem was present to him, and Dante had thereby become *second nature* to him. Dante, in fact, belonged in the rag-and-bone shop of Eliot's middle-ageing heart, and it was from that sad organ, we might say, that all his lyric ladders started.

Heaney was referring here to one of W.B. Yeats' late poems, 'The Circus Animals' Desertion', where Yeats contemplates the drying up of his own poetical inspiration. He concludes that inspiration must come from within the self:

> Now that my ladder's gone,
> I must lie down where all the ladders start,
> In the foul rag-and-bone shop of the heart.

In a similar way, the importance of the Italian poet to Heaney's own work is evident from the number of references and translations which accumulate throughout Heaney's work. As Dante gave a voice to the dead and allowed the political strife of Florence to have a reality in the present, so Heaney's own past and the past of his war-torn country keep reappearing throughout his work. His concern with voices from the past rings out not only from his translation of Baudelaire's 'The Digging Skeleton' ('La Squelette Laboureur') from *North* (1975), but also from the way the bodies of the Bog People are unearthed and presented to the eye in poems from the 1970s such as 'The Grauballe Man'. He had tried his hand at translating Dante with the Ugolino episode from Cantos XXXII and XXXIII of *Inferno* which appears in *Fieldwork* (1979). The haunting centrality of the Italian poet to Heaney is made clear again more recently in 'The Crossing' and 'District and Circle' (see Part 1, page 12).

However, Heaney's interest in translation does not rest with Dante; one of the central poems in *The Spirit Level* is 'Mycenae Lookout', based upon episodes from the trilogy of plays by Aeschylus about the end of the Trojan War, *The Oresteia*. 'Mycenae Lookout', a poem divided into five sections, starts from the viewpoint of the watchman on the wall witnessing the triumphant return of King Agamemnon after the sacking of Troy; it reveals the impotent position of the ordinary citizen caught in the crossfire. Heaney juxtaposes the political resonance of the Greek tragedy with the moment of political hope which occurred in Northern Ireland in September 1994 when the Catholic IRA Provisionals and the Protestant Ulster paramilitaries agreed to a truce. The years of violence and murder seemed about to end and Heaney, who in 'Punishment' (*North*) had written about the girl from the archaeological past who had been ritually executed, could contemplate:

> And then this ladder of our own that ran
> deep into a well-shaft being sunk
> in broad daylight, men puddling at the source
>
> through tawny mud, then coming back up
> deeper in themselves for having been there,
> like discharged soldiers testing the safe ground,
>
> finders, keepers, seers of fresh water
> in the bountiful round mouths of iron pumps
> and gushing taps.
>
> (From 'Mycenae Lookout', 1996)

Seeing Things ends with 'The Crossing', a translation from Canto III of Dante's *Inferno*. It opens with 'The Golden Bough', a translation of part of Book VI of Virgil's *Aeneid*. In this poem, Aeneas plucks the golden bough which allows him not only safe entry to the spirit world of the dead but also a safe return: contemplation of loss can be followed by a return to a hopeful present. Perhaps this reflects some of the attitudes which Heaney expressed about the cessation of violence:

> The cessation of violence is an opportunity to open a space – and not just in the political arena but in the first level of each person's consciousness – a space where hope can grow … Hope, according to Havel, is different from optimism. It is a state of the soul rather than a response to the evidence. It is not the expectation that things will turn out successfully but the conviction that something is worth working for, however it turns out. Its deepest roots are in the transcendental, beyond the horizon. The self-evident truth of all this is surely something upon which a peace process might reasonably be grounded.
>
> (*Sunday Tribune*, September 1994)

Heaney's ability to see the present reflected in the past is also evident in *The Cure at Troy* (1990), his version of Sophocles' play, *Philoctetes*, where personal integrity and political expediency clash in the story of the wounded man left behind by his comrades on the Isle of Lemnos. *The Cure at Troy* opens with lines which can be seen as reflecting not only the political stance of those involved in the Irish question, but also that of all self-righteous political combatants:

> Heroes. Victims. Gods and human beings.
> All throwing shapes, every one of them
> Convinced he's in the right, all of them glad
> To repeat themselves and their every last mistake,
> No matter what.
>
> People so deep into
> Their own self-pity self-pity buoys them up.
> People so staunch and true, they're fixated,
> Shining with self-regard like polished stones.

The extensive range of Heaney's ability as a translator is confirmed most of all with his rendering of the Old English heroic poem, *Beowulf* (1999). According to one reviewer in the *New York Times*, 'This translation does something other than bring him [Beowulf] up into our time. It transports us to his and lets us wander there; after which home will never seem entirely the same.' Heaney's vitality of language in this translation was rewarded by his winning of the Whitbread Prize in 2000, just beating the other main contender, J.K. Rowling.

Michael Hoffmann and James Lasdun highlight the importance of classical literature in the present time:

> Then, too, the stories have direct, obvious and powerful affinities with contemporary reality. They offer a mythical key to most of the more extreme forms of human behavior and suffering, especially ones we think of as peculiarly modern: holocaust, plague, sexual harassment, rape, incest, seduction, pollution, sex-change, suicide, hetero-and homosexual love, torture, war, child-battering, depression and intoxication form the bulk of the themes.
>
> (Introduction to *After Ovid, New Metamorphoses*, 1994)

Ted Hughes contributed four extracts to this volume and the result was so successful that he was asked by Faber to produce a book of translations from *Metamorphoses* which were then published in 1997 as *Tales from Ovid*. In his introduction to that volume, Hughes commented upon 'human passion *in extremis*' and 'an experience of the supernatural' where 'the all-too-human victim stumbles out into the mythic arena and is transformed'.

The perceived importance of Ovid's stories is evidenced by the number of prominent British poets who contributed to the Hoffmann / Lasdun volume: Simon Armitage, Tom Paulin, Fred D'Aguiar, Craig Raine, Peter Reading, Ciaran Carson, Michael Longley, Paul Muldoon, Charles Tomlinson, Seamus Heaney,

Derek Mahon, Carol Ann Duffy, Jo Shapcott, Vicki Feaver. As with any translation, there will always be those academics who feel that the translator has been too concerned with creating poetic effects in a new language: the demands of the 'poet' have come before the exact knowledge of the workings of a different language. However, Ezra Pound did not need an intimate knowledge of Chinese before producing his series of poems in 1915, *Cathay*, among the most moving lyrical pieces of the 20th century.

As referred to in the discussion of 'space' in Part 1 (see page 30), Simon Armitage's introduction to his translation of *Sir Gawain and the Green Knight* (2007) points to another area of interest for the modern poet:

> The lack of authorship seems to serve as an invitation, opening up a space within the poem for a new writer to occupy.

Both Armitage and Heaney have translated work from the British cultural tradition, highlighting the vibrant and alliterative qualities of sound in the English language. In a manner similar to Heaney's *Beowulf*, this new translation of the anonymous Middle-English *Gawain* also has a ringing sound, a resonance of language at work:

> 'This is a haunted house – may it go to hell.
> I never came across a church so cursed.'
> With head helmeted and lance in hand
> he scrambled to the skylight of that strange abyss.
> Then he heard on the hillside, from behind a hard rock
> and beyond the brook, a blood-chilling noise.
> What! It cannoned through the cliffs as if they might crack,
> like the scream of a scythe being ground on a stone.
> What! It whined and wailed, like a waterwheel.
> What! It rasped and rang, raw on the ear.

Black poetry

In 'Black Men's Poetry in Britain', Alistair Niven points to an interesting aspect of cultural tradition:

> It is far more difficult to trace in either the Caribbean or the Indian ancestries of black British poetry a lineage of influence comparable to that which informs most prominent white British poetry of the modern period. This is partly because black expressiveness is more inherently oral than white, which, with rare exceptions, has lost much significant contact with balladry, song, or folk material. It is also, however, evidence of the deracination that lies behind so much black British writing.
>
> (Acheson and Huk *Contemporary British Poetry*, 1996)

In reference to this last point – the sense of being uprooted, of losing one's cultural roots – one might refer to Grace Nichols's 'Epilogue', in the collection *I is a Long-Memoried Woman* (1983):

> I have crossed an ocean
> I have lost my tongue
> from the root of the old one
> a new one has sprung.

However, it is also worth noting the comments made by Paterson and Simic on their inclusion of four of Fred D'Aguiar's poems in *New British Poetry* (published in America in 2004). They suggest that his 'sharp-witted and knowing verse has often circled round questions of culture and identity'. In 'Home' (see Part 3, page 96), the poet plays with the idea of different concepts of the word as he returns to his London home after a time away. Familiar aspects of British life such as a red telephone box assert a nostalgic pull that makes D'Aguiar 'miss here more than anything I can name'. Juxtaposed with the musical expressiveness of the plane's arrival at Heathrow when his heart 'performs a jazzy drum solo' we are presented with the 'chirpily' conversational cockney cab driver who won't 'steer clear of race / so rounds on Asians'. The musical uplift of the way D'Aguiar then diminishes the racist taxi driver demands to be read out loud:

> He settles at the wheel grudgingly,
> in a huffed silence. Cha! Drive man!
> I have legal tender burning in my pocket
> to move on, like a cross in Transylvania.

Identity is also central to Jackie Kay's work as can be seen in 'Pride' (see Part 3, page 97). In her introduction to the selection of her poems in the anthology *New Blood* (1999), she made it clear that 'I will always be interested in identity, how fluid it is, how people can invent themselves, how it can never be fixed or frozen'. Having been adopted and brought up in Scotland, she is conscious of being asked where she is from and says that, 'mixing fact with fiction and trying to illuminate the border country that exists between them', her country is a mixture of many experiences. The central role that the fluidity of music plays is evident in her love of Bessie Smith's blues and the plot of her novel, *Trumpet* (1999), where an apparently male jazz trumpeter turns out to be a woman.

The importance of the oral tradition in its ability to unsettle the mainstream of academic poetry reading was highlighted when Benjamin Zephaniah's name was put forward for a job at Cambridge University. He remains the only Rastafarian to be shortlisted for a professorship at both Oxford and Cambridge, but Alistair Niven notes that:

His application failed for reasons that were not entirely risible, but it became clear that those in the university who pronounced adversely upon his work did so without any knowledge of its Caribbean roots. They paid exclusive regard to the effect of a fixed printed text, because European literary criticism has now raised that above all other values.

In the preface to his collection, *Too Black, Too Strong* (2001), Zephaniah suggests that he is a poet who is not going to remain silent; he has added considerably to the sense of the living and moving quality of verse by having his own reggae band and by committing himself to performance poetry.

Alistair Niven's conclusion to his essay on 'Black Men's Poetry in Britain' places the current situation in a very effective way:

Black British poetry in Britain, from whatever sources it derives, faces acute problems of gaining recognition by the arbiters of equality – the editors of leading literary journals, the chain booksellers, those who set examination syllabi in schools and colleges, those who buy books for libraries out of tight budgets. Its energy, even if strongest when the background is Caribbean, is so vibrant that one must assume that it will grow in reputation and acceptance. It will then perhaps be redundant to call it 'black' at all. Derek Walcott, after all, has commented that no one ever called him a black poet until he received the Nobel Prize, whereupon it became obligatory!

Assignments

1 'Poetry is a dark art, a form of magic, because it tries to change the way we perceive the world' (see above, page 42). Defend or attack Don Paterson's idea that poetry is in any sense a 'magic' art.

2 Compare any two poems by women writers that use dramatic monologue. Does this give the poems greater impact or do you agree with Vicki Feaver that poems are more powerful when they allow the poet to speak with her own voice?

3 Is Tony Harrison's poem *A Cold Coming* best approached as a satire on modern war itself or as a commentary on contemporary attitudes to media reporting of war?

4 How effectively do the translations by Heaney, Hughes and others disprove (or demonstrate the truth of) Robert Frost's claim that 'poetry is what gets lost in translation'?

5 What if anything can mainstream British poetry learn from Black poetry and poets?

3 | Texts and extracts

Vicki Feaver

Many of Vicki Feaver's poems explore the themes of myth and its relationship
with an inner awareness of self. In *How Poets Work*, Feaver suggests that she was
strongly influenced by the confessional mode of writing of the American poet
Sharon Olds. This gave her the courage to use the first person singular rather than
the literary distancing of 'she', a device 'I had used frequently in my first book as
a way of making poems appear less autobiographical. The effect was to split me
off from emotion that allowed into the poem might have given them more energy
and conviction.' 'Judith' deals with the Old Testament story of Judith, the Hebrew
woman who seeks to protect her people from invasion by the Assyrians by killing
their General, Holofernes.

Judith

Wondering how a good woman can murder
I enter the tent of Holofernes,
holding in one hand his long oiled hair
and in the other, raised above
his sleeping, wine-flushed face,
his falchion with its unsheathed
curved blade. And I feel a rush
of tenderness, a longing
to put down my weapon, to lie
sheltered and safe in a warrior's
fumy sweat, under the emerald stars
of his purple and gold canopy,
to melt like a sweet on his tongue
to nothing. And I remember the glare
of the barley field; my husband
pushing away the sponge I pressed
to his burning head; the stubble
puncturing my feet as I ran,
flinging myself on a body
that was already cooling
and stiffening; and the nights
when I lay on the roof – my emptiness
like the emptiness of a temple
with the doors kicked in; and the mornings
when I rolled in the ash of the fire
just to be touched and dirtied

by something. And I bring my blade
down on his neck – and it's easy,
like slicing through fish.
And I bring it down again,
cleaving the bone.

(from The Handless Maiden, 1994)

Yews

Fed on the blood of Vikings,
stained a deep umber red,
trees driven by the passions
of xylem and phloem to break out
of the fastness of wood,
branches twisting into necks,
heads, tusks. Poisoners,
their venom in feathery needles,
in seeds buried in the pulp
of the female's orange berries.

I stand in their smothering tents,
the space where nothing grows,
adjusting to the thin light,
the resinous stillness,
the sleepiness of thinking
this would be the moment
to lie down and die.

(from The Book of Blood, 2006)

Carol Ann Duffy

Carol Ann Duffy's use of dramatic monologue gives women a voice. Duffy's
'women monologists are frequently powerful, vengeful women whose
assertiveness, violence and aggression parodies stereotypes of male behaviour'
(Deryn Rees-Jones in *Consorting with Angels*). 'Little Red-Cap' uses aspects of the
fairytale character of Little Red Riding Hood; in Greek mythology Demeter is the
mother of Persephone, the embodiment of Spring.

Little Red-Cap

At childhood's end, the houses petered out
into playing fields, the factory, allotments
kept, like mistresses, by kneeling married men,
the silent railway line, the hermit's caravan,
till you came at last to the edge of the woods.
It was there that I first clapped eyes on the wolf.

He stood in a clearing, reading his verse out loud
in his wolfy drawl, a paperback in his hairy paw,
red wine staining his bearded jaw. What big ears
he had! What big eyes he had! What teeth!
In the interval, I made quite sure he spotted me,
sweet sixteen, never been, babe, waif, and bought me a drink,

my first. You might ask why. Here's why. Poetry.
The wolf, I knew, would lead me deep into the woods,
away from home, to a dark tangled thorny place
lit by the eyes of owls. I crawled in his wake,
my stockings ripped to shreds, scraps of red from my blazer
snagged on twig and branch, murder clues. I lost both shoes

but got there, wolf's lair, better beware. Lesson one that night,
breath of the wolf in my ear, was the love poem.
I clung till dawn to his thrashing fur, for
what little girl doesn't dearly love a wolf?
Then I slipped from between his heavy matted paws
and went in search of a living bird – white dove –

which flew, straight, from my hands to his open mouth.
One bite, dead. How nice, breakfast in bed, he said,
licking his chops. As soon as he slept, I crept to the back
of the lair, where a whole wall was crimson, gold, aglow with books.
Words, words were truly alive on the tongue, in the head,
warm, beating, frantic, winged; music and blood.

But then I was young – and it took ten years
in the woods to tell that a mushroom
stoppers the mouth of a buried corpse, that birds
are the uttered thought of trees, that a greying wolf
howls the same old song at the moon, year in, year out,
season after season, same rhyme, same reason. I took an axe

to a willow to see how it wept. I took an axe to a salmon
to see how it leapt. I took an axe to the wolf
as he slept, one chop, scrotum to throat, and saw
the glistening, virgin white of my grandmother's bones.
I filled his old belly with stones. I stitched him up.
Out of the forest I come with my flowers, singing, all alone.

(from *The World's Wife*, 1999)

Demeter
Where I lived – winter and hard earth.
I sat in my cold stone room
choosing tough words, granite, flint,

to break the ice. My broken heart –
I tried that, but it skimmed,
flat, over the frozen lake.

She came from a long, long way,
but I saw her at last, walking,
my daughter, my girl, across the fields,

in bare feet, bringing all spring's flowers
to her mother's house. I swear
the air softened and warmed as she moved,

the blue sky smiling, none too soon,
with the small shy mouth of a new moon.

(from *The World's Wife*, 1999)

If I Was Dead

If I was dead,
and my bones adrift
like dropped oars
in the deep, turning earth;

or drowned,
and my skull
a listening shell
on the dark ocean bed;

if I was dead,
and my heart
soft mulch
for a red, red rose;

or burned,
and my body
a fistful of grit, thrown
in the face of the wind;

if I was dead,
and my eyes,
blind at the roots of flowers,
wept into nothing,

I swear your love
would raise me
out of my grave,
in my flesh and blood,

like Lazarus;
hungry for this,
and this, and this,
your living kiss.

(from *Rapture*, 2005)

Carol Rumens

As the editor of *Making for the Open: The Chatto Book of Post-Feminist Poetry* (1985) Rumens suggested that the 'man-made language theory grossly underestimates women's articulateness and their powers of communication, powers which go back far beyond the written word. Is it not rather more likely that those people who throughout history have spent much of their lives talking to children, singing them songs and repeating rhymes to them have played the greater part in the evolution of language, particularly literary language?'

From a Conversation During Divorce
It's cold, you say, the house.
Yes, of course I'll go back one day,
Visit, that is. But the house

Will be cold, just as you say.
Two people have left home,
One of them me, and one

Our youngest child. So of course
It's cold, just as you say,
And big, too, bigger at least

Than it was with everyone there.
Don't think I don't think about you
Being cold in a house that size,

A house that gets bigger, too,
And colder each time I dare
Think about you and the house.

It used to be warm in the days
Before I decided to go,
And it didn't seem big at all,

In fact, it was rather small,
Which is partly the reason I …
Don't keep on asking me why

And telling me how it is
In the house. I don't want to know.
How can I go back, how can I

Even visit a house that size,
And getting bigger each minute
With all the cold rooms in it?

(from *Best China Sky*, 1995)

Elizabeth Cook

'The poems in Elizabeth Cook's most recent volume, enveloped within a delicate diction, insinuate themselves through a reverence for the elemental and those vessels that hold memory. They are substantial, carrying thought above style and image, and yet light, alert to measurement and revelation.' David Caddy (*The Use of English 58,3*)

Bowl
Give me a bowl, wide
and shallow. Patient
to light as a landscape open
to the whole weight
of a deepening sky.

Give me a bowl which turns
for ever on a curve
so gentle a child
could bear it and beasts
lap fearless at its low rim.

(from *Bowl*, 2006)

Seamus Heaney

Both of these poems reveal the powerful influence of Dante referred to in Part 1: they focus on the world of human suffering and the nightmares facing people today.

The Crossing
And there in a boat that came heading towards us
Was an old man, his hair snow-white with age,
Raging and bawling, 'Woe to you, wicked spirits!

O never hope to see the heavenly skies!
I come to bring you to the other shore,
To eternal darkness, to the fire and ice.

And you there, you, the living soul, separate
Yourself from these others who are dead.'
But when he saw that I did not stand aside

He said, 'By another way, by other harbours
You shall reach a different shore and pass over.
A lighter boat must be your carrier.'

And my guide said, 'Quiet your anger, Charon.
There where all can be done that has been willed
This has been willed; so there can be no question.'

Then straightaway he shut his grizzled jaws,
The ferryman of that livid marsh,
Who had wheels of fire flaming round his eyes.

But as soon as they had heard the cruel words,
Those lost souls, all naked and exhausted,
Changed their colour and their teeth chattered;

They blasphemed God and their parents on the earth,
The human race, the place and date and seedbed
Of their own begetting and of their birth,

Then all together, bitterly weeping, made
Their way towards the accursed shore that waits
For every man who does not fear his God.

The demon Charon's eyes are like hot coals fanned.
He beckons them and herds all of them in
And beats with his oar whoever drops behind.

As one by one the leaves fall off in autumn
Until at last the branch is bare and sees
All that was looted from it on the ground,

So the bad seed of Adam, at a signal
Pitch themselves off that shore one by one,
Each like a falcon answering its call.

They go away like this over the brown waters
And before they have landed on the other side
Upon this side once more a new crowd gathers.

'My son,' the courteous master said to me,
'All those who die under the wrath of God
Come together here from every country

And they are eager to go across the river
Because Divine Justice goads them with its spur
So that their fear is turned into desire.

No good spirits ever pass this way
And therefore, if Charon objects to you,
You should understand well what his words imply.'
(Inferno, Canto III, lines 82–129, from Seeing Things, 1991)

District and Circle

Tunes from a tin whistle underground
Curled up a corridor I'd be walking down
To where I knew I was always going to find
My watcher on the tiles, cap by his side,
His fingers perked, his two eyes eyeing me
In an unaccusing look I'd not avoid,
Or not just yet, since both were out to see
For ourselves.
                              As the music larked and capered
I'd trigger and untrigger a hot coin
Held at the ready, but now my gaze was lowered
For was our traffic not in recognition?
Accorded passage, I would re-pocket and nod,
And he, still eyeing me, would also nod.

~

Posted, eyes front, along the dreamy ramparts
Of escalators ascending and descending
To a monotonous slight rocking in the works,
We were moved along, upstanding.
Elsewhere, underneath, an engine powered,
Rumbled, quickened, evened, quieted.
The white tiles gleamed. In passages that flowed
With draughts from cooler tunnels, I missed the
    light
Of all-overing, long since mysterious day,
Parks at lunchtime where the sunners lay
On body-heated mown grass regardless,
A resurrection scene minutes before
The resurrection, habitués
Of their garden of delights, of staggered summer.

~

Another level down, the platform thronged.
I re-entered the safety of numbers,

A crowd half straggle-ravelled and half strung
Like a human chain, the pushy newcomers
Jostling and purling underneath the vault,
On their marks to be first through the doors,
Street-loud, then succumbing to herd-quiet...
Had I betrayed or not, myself or him?
Always new to me, always familiar,
This unrepentant, now repentant turn
As I stood waiting, glad of a first tremor,
Then caught up in the now-or-never whelm
Of one and all the full length of the train.

~

Stepping on to it across the gap,
On to the carriage metal, I reached to grab
The stubby black roof-wort and take my stand
From planted ball of heel to heel of hand
As sweet traction and heavy down-slump stayed me.
I was on my way, well girded, yet on edge,
Spot-rooted, buoyed, aloof,
Listening to the dwindling noises off,
My back to the unclosed door, the platform empty;
And wished it could have lasted,
That long between-times pause before the budge
And glaze-over, when any forwardness
Was unwelcome and bodies readjusted,
Blindsided to themselves and other bodies.

~

So deeper into it, crowd-swept, strap-hanging,
My lofted arm a-swivel like a flail,
My father's glazed face in my own waning
And craning ...
                    Again the growl
Of shutting doors, the jolt and one-off treble
Of iron on iron, then a long centrifugal
Haulage of speed through every dragging socket.

And so by night and day to be transported
Through galleried earth with them, the only relict
Of all that I belonged to, hurtled forward,
Reflecting in a window mirror-backed
By blasted weeping rock-walls.
                    Flicker-lit.

(from *District and Circle*, 2006)

Andrew Crozier

Crozier's 'The Veil Poem' was one of the central **metaphysical** sequences from the 1970s. This is a more recent poem.

Blank Misgivings

Our father death speaks through the child our father
the sailor lost beside a dream of immense steppes
perfectly rigged violets inside a sunken bottle
tears condensed beneath the clear glass in the path

O fly you creatures, asiatic cranes and gazelles
slender ribbed of arctic birch and whalebone
air twists into grey sheets of old starlight
the extinct hiss of incendiary in a bombed cellar

This morning's trace of footprints leads back where
sidereal years modelled in spars and struts
thrust from the ground, stumps of brickwork
a broken corner where the sky turns cold

Remember such things under the new city
shadows of ruin swept into unlit night
one bare horizon drawn across another
day into day breaks the calamity of the heart

What to call to out of ignorance and loved best
the abrupt twilight and the unexpected dawn
when brief cries summon falls unanswering voice
pauses between the echoes of the century

Listen to the wagons thunder and the static roar
light outlined burning through the grid
the abandoned garden and the tumbled fence
alike and other unbuilt monuments to hope

The stones rest as they fall, the dying fall
among the dead and I could wish their bones
at rest their day so what there was each find
so be it the unhoped-for be no more than man

(from 'Gare du Nord', 1998,
reprinted in *Vanishing Points*, 2004)

Barry MacSweeney

In the haunting *Pearl* sequence, MacSweeney celebrates his feelings for a mute girl whom he had taught to read in the fields of Sparty Lea in Northumberland.

Pearl's Utter Brilliance

Argent moon with bruised shawl
discreetly shines upon my frozen tongue tonight
and I am grinning handclap glad.
We loved so much the lunar light
on rawbone law or splashing in the marigold beds,
our gazing faces broken in the stream.
Taut, not taught, being kept from school
was a disgrace, single word 'idiot' chalked
on the yard wall: soaked in sleet, sliding
in snow beneath a raft of sighs, waiting
for the roar of an engine revved before
daybreak, as the world, the permanent wound
I would never know in sentence construction, fled
away from my heather-crashing feet, splash happy
kneefalls along the tumblestones,
whip-winged plovers shattering the dew.
Each day up here I am fiercely addressed
by the tips of the trees; said all I could
while heifers moaned in the stalls, clopping
of hooves my steaming, shitting
beast accompaniment. And these giant clouds.
Pity? Put it in the slurry with the rest of your woes.
I am Pearl, queen of the dale.

(from *Wolf Tongue*, 2003)

Pearl Alone

Yes, I am not emitting articulate sound.
I take my stand and – deliberately – refuse to plead.
There is no adoration in my mute appeal.
My tongue a pad or cone for the trumpet's bell.
Tongue-tied, bereft of ABC, I lap
and soak my whistle at the law's rim.
In mood moments
I say smash down the chalkboard:
let it stay black.
Shake my chained tongue, I'll fake a growl – a-a-a-a-a-.
Dog my steps, I am wet-toed to the spring
for mam's tea: spam on Sundays
and chips if there is coal.

In the Orient I would be a good servant
willing to please.
Damping of strings my speciality,
an hired mourner
for the rest of my days: gazer
at umbrellas and rain.
No use for owt else up here
except wiping my legs of heifer muck
and fetching the four o'clock milk.
In the byre alone I weep
at the imagined contrivance
of straps and wires
locking my loll-tongue gargoyle head.
My muzzle gushes rain
and I wince when people speak to mam,
giving me their sideways look.
My eyes go furious and I stamp, stamp, stamp.
Pulse fever even in Hartfell sleet.
Loud tumult, what there is of my mind
tumbled into the lashing trees. Yes,
I love falling, caught momentarily
through each tall command of branches, amazed once more
at the borage blue sky
in another September afternoon
with tongue spouting, soaking the cones, thudding
to the very ground, disturbing
all the birds and worms and wasps and bees.
Don't count on me for fun
among the towering cowslips,
but please don't crush my heart.

(from *Wolf Tongue*, 2003)

I Looked Down on a Child Today

I looked down on a child today, not because he or she was smaller than me
or because I was being in my middle-aged way fatherless and
        condescending
but because he or she was dying or dead between the kerbstone and the
        wheel

I stepped down from the steps of a 39 bus today with sudden blood on
        my shoes
The lesions and lessons and the languorous long-winged stiff-winged
        fulmars
chalked against the sky and white against the unpainted lips of her

I looked down at a child today, Gallowgate, the bus was turning left
the child stepped out, leaving its mam's hand behind partly swept by the
wind
and partly by blind wonderful enthusiasm for life we guard against
increasingly

She stepped into the path of something she or he would never know
forever
In an elegant but unassuming place where as a living they hanged
prisoners for bread-theft
It was the eve of St Valentine's Day on the wild side of Geordieland

The white dresses were being collected from dry cleaners Darn Crook to
Sidgate
the strategy of the masses was being unaddressed once more except
through the tills
where paper receipts come clicking out increasingly slowly to everyone's
annoyance

What a beautiful, brilliant day, tart with expectation of love and romance
in Chinatown
or down the Bigg Market as lager casks were moved into station and the
dance floors cleaned
I looked down at a child today, never having had one of my own, and
having no kid

I can call mine in a very old-fashioned romantic Barry MacSweeney Elvis
Orbison Highway 61 way
O Robert it was almost where you left on the bus O Aaron O Dusty O
Blackened Eyelids
I looked down upon a child today under the buswheels and knew
whatever your name you would see

heaven and it would shine and be filled with pianos and trumpets and not
be suppressed
and freedom would be written in moth-dust on every angel's wings
and there will be the music of Shostakovich and Poulenc when you wanted
to hear it

and the monumental poetry of MacDiarmid and Mahon and all spirits
would gather there
and tell you when you awake again what lemonbalm was and you and say
I looked down on a child and bonnybairn in blood today the day before St
Valentine's Day

(from *Wolf Tongue*, 2003)

Anthony Wilson

Anthony Wilson's article 'Poets I Go Back To' (*The North* 39, 2006) opens uncompromisingly with the line 'Last February I discovered I had cancer'. The article concludes that to him the most important recent poetry 'returns me to the business of living with fresh eyes, fresh hopes and with new and exciting phrases to chew on and memorise without knowing it'.

Prac Crit

The first thing is to read the poem several times.
That way you become familiar with the text.
Not one study guide ever published can replace
the virtue of *the words themselves*. Make notes

as you go along, in the margin. Underline things.
Write down what succeeds. Analyse the poet's
technique. Is it rhymed and does it have metre?
Does it correspond to a pattern, *abab*, for example,

or a sonnet? If not, is it free verse, or *vers libre*?
Form is all very well but if it's not married to content
the poem will fail as Art. Then to the actual material.
Take the nouns. Are they solid – or abstract?

Door is of the solid kind, *fear* of the abstract.
Thus, a poem about a door might really be about
fear. Watch out for this. It is called imagery.
Then take a look at the verbs. The verbs

are a poem's engine. Do they push the poem along
or do they hold it back? Also, the adjectives.
An adjective must work like a muscle, very hard.
If it doesn't, it shouldn't be there. A poem which

contains the word *nice*, for example, is nearly always
bad. Finally, what is the poem about? Does it
contain nudity, or references to young boys?
How is the poet using them, to explore his feelings,

or does he have other ideas? If blackmail
is involved it's possible the poem is in code.
Anyone with problems in this area should see me
afterwards. The door to my study's never closed.

(from *Full Stretch*, 2006)

Charles Tomlinson

In conversation with Jordi Doce in 1995, Charles Tomlinson said: 'I think my poetry is extremely physical in the way it moves and it has a melodic continuity – rather like the way an aria advances, pauses, takes up a theme once more, puts it aside, returns to it and so on. The bodily involvement also has its parallel with the involvement of hand and eye in painting – that sense of exquisite physical contact you feel in using a paint brush or in drawing – replicated on a cruder level in what is for me the groundwork of poetry.' (*Agenda Vol. 33 No 2*) 'In A Cambridge Garden' is dedicated to the Mexican poet and Nobel Prize winner, Octavio Paz, at a time when both men were contemplating the possibility of taking up posts in foreign countries: Paz in England and Tomlinson in America.

In a Cambridge Garden
Another town and time – and little left of it
      Before you were to go. Castles in Spain
Stood solid to receive your royal progress
      While Wren detained us. Beyond his colonnade
Arched and shaded, as if Italian paviours
      Had laid the flags we echoed on – our way
Led us to lawns whose midday shadows
      Seemed cast from trees as massive
I was about to say, as those that grow
      In Mexico itself – but no: this plane,
This copper beech, both take their scale
      From their own setting, and could stand
Nowhere but here, their power contained
      Beside a wall in England. Had you stayed on
Twenty years ago, had I gone
      To live in the house at Nine Mile Swamp,
My children would have been Americans, and you
      An exotic in this Cambridge garden. Now
These inquests on past possibilities
      Serve merely to say that we
Were right to choose the differing parsimonies
      Of the places we belonged to. I thought
That I could teach my countrymen to see
      The changing English light, like water
That drips off a gunwale driving through the sea,
      Showing the way the whole world
Dipping through space and cloud and sun,
      Surges across the day as it travels on
Turning. In short, I stayed. Your life,

Pitted against the rigid summa
Of Thomists turned politicians, grew
    More public every year, and mine
In its privacy, more sociable, perhaps,
    Than one that contemplates that upstate view
Over uninhabited acres blank with snow.
    What would you have missed the most?
First, I know, would have come colour.
    We cannot pretend our island exhalations
Do not douse the harshness of that clarity
    That burns back in ochres, oranges and reds
Off Mexican walls. The ground beneath them
    Wears a brown Franciscan serge –
Not drab, because seen at first intensity
    Under such a light. Some, I suppose,
– Not you – might find the colours of a place
    Small reason for living there –
It took an Englishman (John Locke),
    Meagre and precise, to call them 'secondary'.
And here, fanaticism and moderation meet –
    I think when Mercader killed Trotsky,
The colours of that garden in Coyoacan
    Counted for little: he hurried through
Drawn by the thought of what it was he'd do,
    Senses sheered back to its accomplishment.
So you returned. To the monoxide monotony
    That taints the trees of Mixcoac –
'There *are* no gardens,' as you said, 'except
    For those we carry with us.' Now we, too,
Must hurry through the hospitality
    Of this one, ready for the car
(The gates are opening) that awaits you
    (And the street looks in.) And so we coincide
Against distance, wind and tide, meet
    And translate our worlds to one another,
Greet in verse. A poem is itself
    A sort of garden – we are waving our farewells –
Seasonable at all times as we bring
    Our changing seasons to it – we are losing sight
Of the speeding car that is launched and one
    With the traffic now and the mid-May sun.

(from *The Door in the* Wall, 1992)

Ted Hughes

After the publication of *Birthday Letters* (1998), Hughes wrote to friend and critic, Keith Sagar, that the poems were confessional in a style that he had 'always thought unthinkable – so raw, so vulnerable, so naive, so self-exposing and unguarded, so without any of the niceties that any poetry workshop student could have helped me to'. 'Visit' is based upon an incident that took place soon after Hughes and Sylvia Plath first met. Hughes and his friend Lucas Myers went into the grounds of Newnham College, Cambridge, to wake her up one night by flinging mud up at her window. However, it was the wrong window and she was out that night anyway. In her diary she wrote about the incident: 'He is on the prowl, all the fiends are come to torment me … last night they came, at two in the morning, Phillippa said. Throwing mud on her window, saying my name, the two mixed: mud and my name; my name is mud.'

Visit

Lucas, my friend, one
Among those three or four who stay unchanged
Like a separate self,
A stone in the bed of the river
Under every change, became your friend.
I heard of it, alerted. I was sitting
Youth away in an office near Slough,
Morning and evening between Slough and Holborn,
Hoarding wage to fund a leap to freedom
And the other side of the earth – a free-fall
To strip my chrysalis off me in the slipstream.
Weekends I recidived
Into Alma Mater. Girl-friend
Shared a supervisor and weekly session
With your American rival and you.
She detested you. She fed snapshots
Of you and she did not know what
Inflammable celluloid into my silent
Insatiable future, my blind-man's-buff
Internal torch of search. With my friend,
After midnight, I stood in a garden
Lobbing soil-clods up at a dark window.

Drunk, he was certain it was yours.
Half as drunk, I did not know he was wrong.
Nor did I know I was being auditioned
For the male lead in your drama,
Miming through the first easy movements

As if with eyes closed, feeling for the role.
As if a puppet were being tried on its strings,
Or a dead frog's legs touched by electrodes.
I jigged through those gestures – watched and judged
Only by starry darkness and a shadow.
Unknown to you and not knowing you.
Aiming to find you, and missing, and again missing.
Flinging earth at a glass that could not protect you
Because you were not there.

Ten years after your death
I meet on a page of your journal, as never before,
The shock of your joy
When you heard of that. Then the shock
Of your prayers. And under those prayers your panic
That prayers might not create the miracle,
Then, under the panic, the nightmare
That came rolling to crush you:
Your alternative – the unthinkable
Old despair and the new agony
Melting into one familiar hell.

Suddenly I read all this –
Your actual words, as they floated
Out through your throat and tongue and onto your page –
Just as when your daughter, years ago now,
Drifting in, gazing up into my face,
Mystified,
Where I worked alone
In the silent house, asked, suddenly:
'Daddy, where's Mummy?' The freezing soil
Of the garden, as I clawed it.
All round me that midnight's
Giant clock of frost. And somewhere
Inside it, wanting to feel nothing,
A pulse of fever. Somewhere
Inside that numbness of the earth
Our future trying to happen.
I look up – as if to meet your voice
With all its urgent future
That has burst in on me. Then look back
At the book of the printed words.
You are ten years dead. It is only a story.
Your story. My story.

(from Birthday Letters, 1998)

R.F. Langley

The background to the poem is a phone call made by Langley's wife to her daughter to find out if she had had her baby. An owl is sitting on the telephone pole and the call won't go through properly: 'Jane couldn't hear us, but we could hear her. So that there was this peculiar – Jane's voice actually in the air, in Suffolk, in the dusk, with an owl sitting looking and Jane unable to hear what we were saying.'

Man Jack

So Jack's your man, Jack is your man in things.
And he must come along, and he must stay
close, be quick and right, your little cousin
Jack, a step ahead, deep in the hedge, on
edge, a kiss a rim, at pinch, in place, turn
face and tip a brim, each inch of him, the
folded leaf, the important straw. What for.
He's slippery and hot. He slides in blood.
Those lies he tells you, running alongside.
To and fro he ducks, and miserably
clicks and puckers up, and in his rage he
won't speak out, or only half. He's short. He's
dim. He'll clench his jaw. He's more than you can
take. He'll drop it all across the road and
spit and go. Over the years you'll have to
learn to pull him in and let him know. You'll
say, 'Today we'll have that, now, those other
apples. So. Oh, but you'll fetch them like I
seem to think I dreamed you did, and they'll be
like they always should have been, in action,
apples in the apples, apples' apples,
through and through.' And then you'll see what he can
do. He'll fetch them in and put them roughly
in a row. The scent will almost be a presence
in the room. 'Oh, but it hurt,' he'll say, 'to
pick across the stones, the different stones.
So many different pains.' Oh Jack. You
hick. You grig. You hob. You Tom, and what not,
with your moans! Your bones are rubber. Get back
out and do it all again. For all the
world an ape! For all the world Tom poke, Tom
tickle and Tom joke! Go back and carry
logs into the hall. And wait with lifted
finger till the eave drops fall. Your task. The

jewel discovered by the monkey in
the shine. Fetch that, and make it much, and mine.
Sometimes it's best if I forget to ask.
An errand boy with nothing up his sleeve,
who stops to listen to the rigmarole
to find he cannot leave without he's bought
the dog. Time out of mind. Just bring
what you can find. Apples. Twigs. Icicles.
Pigs. The owl that watches as we try a
phonecall from the isolated box. Jane's
disembodied voice. The owl that hears her
words. The moon that thinks about her baby.
Jack in the moon. Jane in Jill. The baby
coming sure and soon and bright and staring
at the apples which keep still. The owl had
no idea. More knew Tom fool. The apples
shine in everybody's eyes. Tom speaks
inside his cheeks. The moon talks from inside
his belly. The isolation sighs to think
of motherhood. We hear Jane's tiny words,
as does the owl, astonished, listening
in the roadside wood. Jack gleeks inside
his only box of tricks for what has come.
All thumbs, he Tibs his Tom. It's apples and
it's owls. He bobs and chops and nips until
it's Jill engaged in paradise, with the
enchanted pips. Just in the nick with
only magic left. No use at all to
look at him as if he were a jug. As
if he were. A twig is evidently
a love bouquet. The apples are a gift.
The spellbound owl sits round as such
upon a shelf. Its silence cries out loud
as if you touched it on a wound. It is
embarrassed and delighted with what Jack
has found. And that it had, itself, the wit
required to secretly decipher it.
Until there is a sudden dip into
a silence in the silence, and the owl
has turned his head away and, frightened, stepped
off on his long legs into air, into
an emptiness, left by Jack who is not
there. He's gone too far. Though nothing drops, there's

nothing caught. The twig is two. The gleek is
three. There'd be a mournival in the four
but no one's counting any more. It stops.
The apple is not fire. And yellow is
not sweet. Jane's voice from miles away is just
a speck and almost lost, but yet it is
distinctly Jane, uninfluenced by the moon
she has not seen, the roadside where she has
not been, the owl who thought to pick a peck,
the apples she will never eat. The Jane
who cannot tell us yet the baby's name.
And, undeclared like that, it wins the game.

(from *Collected Poems*, 2000)

David Caddy

When David Caddy was asked about Willy Weekes, the central figure in his 2004
collection, *The Willy Poems*, he replied that 'Willy was the marginal figure. He
appeared in Stourpaine, a lonely, dishevelled and unemployed figure that frightened
the middle class villagers … He had lived all his life at Sturminster Newton and was
not really at home in new surroundings. He was effectively trying to find himself.
It did not work out. Deaths in the family, loss of home and work, had taken him
elsewhere. The only familiar face was mine. And I was not the kid of our joint past.
He drifted in and out of the village and was soon gone.'

The Atmosphere
There's a grating to my mind
hit upon the ground's anvil
above history's particles,
torn and brittle in scope.

And so we have a measurement,
to be resisted, spaces churned,
like the field that runs counter
to its fence, to be nourished.

Entering those dark crevices
that are to die for, to be sustained,
as the man located on the edge
between two views and looking.

I mean to say a friction,
insubstantial echoes of spent lives,
a presence of hands and seeds,
an uncovering of branch and root.

No more than disturbed production
beyond erosion, the weir's roar.
No more than patterns of light
repair where the ash once stood.

(from *The Willy Poems*, 2004)

Tony Harrison

Tony Harrison's *A Cold Coming* was written during the First Gulf War (1991). It takes its title from T.S. Eliot's poem, 'Journey of the Magi' which tells the story of the three Magi visiting the newborn Jesus in Bethlehem. Eliot's poem questions whether the journey of the Magi was to do with birth or death, since the adoption of a new belief would inevitably lead to the death of their old beliefs. Harrison wrote his poem in response to the photograph in the *Guardian* of a charred Iraqi soldier on the road to Basra.

A Cold Coming

I saw the charred Iraqi lean
towards me from bomb-blasted screen,

his windscreen wiper like a pen
ready to write down thoughts for men,

his windscreen wiper like a quill
he's reaching for to make his will.

I saw the charred Iraqi lean
like someone made of Plasticine

as though he'd stopped to ask the way
and this is what I heard him say:

'Don't be afraid I've picked on you
for this exclusive interview.

Isn't it your sort of poet's task
to find words for this frightening mask?

If that gadget that you've got records
words from such scorched vocal chords,

press RECORD before some dog
devours me mid-monologue.'

So I held the shaking microphone
closer to the crumbling bone:

'I read the news of three wise men
who left their sperm in nitrogen,

three foes of ours, three wise Marines
with sample flasks and magazines,

three wise soldiers from Seattle
who banked their sperm before the battle.

Did No. 1 say: God be thanked
I've got my precious semen banked.

And No. 2: O praise the Lord
my last best shot is safely stored.

And No. 3: Praise be to God
I left my wife my frozen wad?

So if their fate was to be gassed
at least they thought their name would last,

and though cold corpses in Kuwait
they could by proxy procreate.

Excuse a skull half roast, half bone
for using such a scornful tone.

It may seem out of all proportion
but I wish I'd taken their precaution.

They seemed the masters of their fate
with wisely jarred ejaculate.

Was it a propaganda coup
to make us think they'd cracked death too,

disinformation to defeat us
with no post-mortem millilitres?

Symbolic billions in reserve
made me, for one, lose heart and nerve.

On Saddam's pay we can't afford
to go and get our semen stored.

Sad to say that such high tech's
uncommon here. We're stuck with sex.

If you can conjure up and stretch
your imagination (and not retch)

the image of me beside my wife
closely clasped creating life …

(I let the unfleshed skull unfold
a story I'd been already told,

and idly tried to calculate
the content of ejaculate:

the sperm in one ejaculation
equals the whole Iraqi nation

times, roughly, let's say, 12.5
though that .5's not now alive.

Let's say the sperms were an amount
so many times the body count,

2,500 times at least
(but let's wait till the toll's released!).

Whichever way Death seems outflanked
by one tube of cold bloblings banked.

Poor bloblings, maybe you've been blessed
with, of all fates possible, the best

according to Sophocles i.e.
'the best of fates is not to be'

a philosophy that's maybe bleak
for any but an ancient Greek

but difficult these days to escape
when spoken to by such a shape.

When you see men brought to such states
who wouldn't want that 'best of fates'

or in the world of Cruise and Scud
not go kryonic if he could,

spared the normal human doom
of having made it through the womb?)

He heard my thoughts and stopped the spool:
'I never thought life futile, fool!

Though all Hell began to drop
I never wanted life to stop.

I was filled with such a yearning
to stay in life as I was burning,

such a longing to be beside
my wife in bed before I died,

and, most, to have engendered there
a child untouched by war's despair.

So press RECORD! I want to reach
the warring nations with my speech.

Don't look away! I know it's hard
to keep regarding one so charred,

so disfigured by unfriendly fire
and think it once burned with desire.

Though fire has flayed off half my features
they once were like my fellow creatures',

till some screen-gazing crop-haired boy
from Iowa or Illinois,

equipped by ingenious technophile
put paid to my paternal smile

and made the face you see today
an armature half-patched with clay,

an icon framed, a looking glass
for devotees of "kicking ass",

a mirror that returns the gaze
of victors on their victory days

and in the end stares out the watcher
who ducks behind his headline: GOTCHA!

or behind the flag-bedecked page 1
of the true to bold-type-setting SUN!

I doubt victorious Greeks let Hector
join their feast as spoiling spectre,

and who'd want to sour the children's joy
in Iowa or Illinois

or ageing mothers overjoyed
to find their babies weren't destroyed?

But cabs beflagged with SUN front pages
don't help peace in future ages.

Stars and Stripes in sticky paws
may sow the seeds for future wars.

Each Union Jack the kids now wave
may lead them later to the grave.

But praise the Lord and raise the banner
(excuse a skull's sarcastic manner!)

Desert Rat and Desert Stormer
without scars and (maybe) trauma,

the semen-bankers are all back
to sire their children in the sack.

With seed sown straight from the sower
dump second-hand spermatozoa!

Lie that you saw me and I smiled
to see the soldier hug his child.

Lie and pretend that I excuse
my bombing by B52s,

pretend I pardon and forgive
that they still do and I don't live,

pretend they have the burnt man's blessing
and then, maybe, I'm spared confessing

that only fire burnt out the shame
of things I'd done in Saddam's name,

the deaths, the torture and the plunder
the black clouds all of us are under.

Say that I'm smiling and excuse
the Scuds we launched against the Jews.

Pretend I've got the imagination
to see the world beyond one nation.

That's your job, poet, to pretend
I want my foe to be my friend.

It's easier to find such words
for this dumb mask like baked dogturds.

So lie and say the charred man smiled
To see the soldier hug his child.

This gaping rictus once made glad
a few old hearts back in Baghdad,

hearts growing older by the minute
as each truck comes without me in it.

I've met you though, and had my say
which you've got taped. Now go away.'

I gazed at him and he gazed back
staring right through me to Iraq.

Facing the way the charred man faced
I saw the frozen phial of waste,

a test-tube frozen in the dark,
crib and Kaaba, sacred Ark,

a pilgrimage of Cross and Crescent
the chilled suspension of the Present.

Rainbows seven shades of black
curved from Kuwait back to Iraq,

and instead of gold the frozen crock's
crammed with Mankind on the rocks,

the congealed genie who won't thaw
until the World renounces War,

cold spunk meticulously jarred
never to be charrer or the charred,

a bottled Bethlehem of this come-
curdling Cruise/Scud-cursed millennium.

I went. I pressed REWIND and PLAY
and I heard the charred man say:

(1991)

Robert Minhinnick

This poem was written after a visit to the Amariya shelter, Baghdad, in 1998. It had been targeted by a smart-bomb in the first Gulf War and four hundred people were burned to death.

The Tooth
(Amariya, Baghdad)

In your head I whisper:
A tooth, blue as a cinder
And I ask: Coward,
Whose pain is it anyway?
Your cells are a blizzard,
Your mind a ragbook, yet
I dream you into growth
Luscious as papaya flesh
Around my black seed.

Why this need to condemn?
I have felt your bones
Gasp in their foundry,
And at night you do not know
But I have heard your blood
Like a bench of silversmiths
Pause at its work.
Then continue.

Once I dreamed
You inside a laboratory
When you stared at a kernel of phosphorous
Until it sprouted fire;
And thirty years later
Ached in your skull
As you stooped in the shelter
Of Amariya to pick the tooth
Of a child like a rice grain
From the ash.

We've been together
Such a long time now.
And my roots
Go all the way down.

(from *100 Poets Against the War*, 2003)

Roy Fisher

Fisher described 'They Come Home' as a 'straight autobiographical piece … about my wife Joyce's parents who had died within a fortnight of each other in 1980' and whose ashes had been brought home from the crematorium to be buried in the garden.

They Come Home
To win back the parents
from the passage-laws;
bring them home together,
bury them under a tree;

spread their bone-dust,
that now stares back at the sun
for the first time and not for long,
two colours of dry limestone,
female and male,
met for the first time, your
fingers and mine mixing your dead
in a layer across the topsoil,
set with corms,
aconite and crocus,
directly under a double-winged
trapdoor of live turf;

by no means separate the dead
from anything.

To have them
won back, by awkward custom;
lifted free
of the crematorium counter
and out from the poor
vestige of common ceremony;

left to our own devices, holding them,
each in a stout paper bag that
covers a squarefaced container
of dull plastic, coloured like
milky cocoa, with a toning beige lid.

And the last journey of all, of necessity
by way of the car-exhaust workshop;

they travel, your foot steadying them upright,
together on the floor, concentrated,
come down to owl-size in their jars,

and they stay there for an hour without us,
lifted up high on the greased, shining
hydraulic pillars under the workshop roof-lights,
closed in my grey-green car
while its rusted and burnt-out piping gets
yanked off and replaced. They come home
over a new smell of hot metal.

By no means separate
from anything at all.

Jars and their paper bags,
name-labels,
go to the bin, with the clearings out
from the discontinued kitchen;

each has still
a whisper of human dust that
clings to the plastic,
the boundary a mad
regress beyond the microscopic.

They're going again in a day or two:

to be in part twice-burned
in city flames; eight hundred
degrees of the lance-burner
under the oven's
brick arch, and then whatever
blast of the municipality
lifts the remainder haze clear of Sheffield
and over the North Sea.

(from Birmingham River, 1994)

Going

When the dead in your generation are still few,
as they go, they reach back; for a while
they fill the whole place with themselves,
rummaging about, inquisitive,
turning everybody on; bringing
their eyes behind yours to make you see things for them.

Now there are more, more every year,
sometimes a month packed full with them
passing through, first dulled, preoccupied, and then
taken quickly to silence. And they're gone, that's all.

(from Birmingham River, 1994)

Charles Olson

Charles Olson's essay 'Projective Verse' (1950) became the most important document concerning an open style of poetry writing.

Projective Verse

First, some simplicities that a man learns, if he works in OPEN, or what can also be called COMPOSITION BY FIELD, as opposed to inherited line, stanza, over-all form, what is the 'old' base of the non-projective.

(1) the *kinetics* of the thing. A poem is energy transferred from where the poet got it (he will have some several causations), by way of the poem itself to, all the way over to, the reader. Okay. Then the poem itself must, at all points, be a high energy-construct and, at all points, an energy-discharge.

(2) is the *principle*, the law which presides conspicuously over such composition, and, when obeyed, is the reason why a projective poem can come into being. It is this: FORM IS NEVER MORE THAN AN EXTENSION OF CONTENT.

(3) the *process* of the thing, how the principle can be made so to shape the energies that the form is accomplished. And I think it can be boiled down to one statement: ONE PERCEPTION MUST IMMEDIATELY AND DIRECTLY LEAD TO A FURTHER PERCEPTION. It means exactly what it says, is a matter of, at *all* points, (even, I should say, of our management of daily reality as of the daily work) get on with it, keep moving, keep in, speed, the nerves, their speed, the perceptions, theirs, the acts, the split second acts, the whole business, keep it moving as fast as you can, citizen. And if you also set up as a poet, USE USE USE the process at all points, in any given poem always, always one perception must must must MOVE, INSTANTER, ON ANOTHER!

(from *The New American Poetry 1945–60*, 1960)

Fred D'Aguiar

Fred D'Aguiar was born in London in 1960, spent much of his childhood in Guyana and now teaches at the University of Miami. In the introduction to the selection of his work in *New British Poetry*, the editors suggest that his mature style 'owes as much to the influence of Tony Harrison and Seamus Heaney as to other Caribbean writers'.

Home

These days whenever I stay away too long,
anything I happen to clap eyes on,
(that red telephone box) somehow makes me
miss here more than anything I can name.

My heart performs a jazzy drum solo
when the crow's feet on the 747
scrape down at Heathrow. H.M. Customs …
I resign to the usual inquisition,

telling me with Surrey loam caked
on the tongue, home is always elsewhere.
I take it like an English middleweight
with a questionable chin, knowing

my passport photo's too open-faced,
haircut wrong (an afro) for the decade;
the stamp, British Citizen, not bold enough
for my liking and too much for theirs.

The cockney cab driver begins chirpily
but can't or won't steer clear of race,
so rounds on Asians. I lock eyes with him
in the rearview when I say I live with one.

He settles at the wheel grudgingly,
in a huffed silence. Cha! Drive man!
I have legal tender burning in my pocket
to move on, like a cross in Transylvania.

At my front door, why doesn't the lock
recognise me and budge? I give an extra
twist and fall forward over the threshold
piled with the felicitations of junk mail,

into a cool reception in the hall.
Grey light and close skies I love you.
Chokey streets, roundabouts and streetlamps
with tyres chucked round them, I love you.

Police officer, your boots need re-heeling.
Robin Redbreast, special request – a burst
of song so the worm can wind to the surface.
We must all sing for our suppers or else.

(from *British Subjects*, 1993)

Jackie Kay

Jackie Kay introduced the selection of her poems published in the anthology *New Blood* (1999) by stating that she would always be interested in identity, 'how fluid it is, how people can invent themselves, how it can never be fixed or frozen'.

Pride

When I looked up, the black man was there,
staring into my face,
as if he had always been there,
as if he and I went a long way back.
He looked into the dark pool of my eyes
as the train slid out of Euston.
For a long time this went on
the stranger and I looking at each other,
a look that was like something being given
from one to the other.

My whole childhood, I'm quite sure,
passed before him, the worst things
I've ever done, the biggest lies I've ever told.
And he was a little boy on a red dust road.
He stared into the dark depth of me,
and then he spoke:
'Ibo,' he said. 'Ibo, definitely.'
Our train rushed through the dark.
'You are an Ibo!' he said, thumping the table.
My coffee jumped and spilled.
Several sleeping people woke.
The night train boasted and whistled
through the English countryside,
past unwritten stops in the blackness.

'That nose is an Ibo nose.
Those teeth are Ibo teeth,' the stranger said,
his voice getting louder and louder.
I had no doubt, from the way he said it,
that Ibo noses are the best noses in the world,
that Ibo teeth are perfect pearls.
People were walking down the trembling aisle
to come and look
as the night rain babbled against the window.
There was a moment when
my whole face changed into a map,

and the stranger on the train
located even the name
of my village in Nigeria
in the lower part of my jaw.

I told him what I'd heard was my father's name.
Okafor. He told me what it meant,
something stunning,
something so apt and astonishing.
Tell me, I asked the black man on the train
who was himself transforming,
at roughly the same speed as the train,
and could have been
at any stop, my brother, my father as a young man,
or any member of my large clan,
Tell me about the Ibos.

His face had a look
I've seen on a MacLachlan, a MacDonnell, a MacLeod,
the most startling thing, pride,
a quality of being certain.
Now that I know you are an Ibo, we will eat.
He produced a spicy meat patty,
ripping it into two.
Tell me about the Ibos.
'The Ibos are small in stature
Not tall like the Yoruba or Hausa.
The Ibos are clever, reliable,
dependable, faithful, true.
The Ibos should be running Nigeria.
There would be none of this corruption.'

And what, I asked, are the Ibos faults?
I smiled my newly acquired Ibo smile,
flashed my gleaming Ibo teeth.
The train grabbed at a bend,
'Faults? No faults. Not a single one.'

'If you went back,' he said brightening,
'The whole village would come out for you.
Massive celebrations. Definitely.
Definitely,' he opened his arms wide.
'The eldest grandchild – fantastic welcome.
If the grandparents are alive.'

CONTEMPORARY POETRY

I saw myself arriving
the hot dust, the red road,
the trees heavy with other fruits,
the bright things, the flowers.
I saw myself watching
the old people dance towards me
dressed up for me in happy prints.
And I found my feet.
I started to dance.
I danced a dance I never knew I knew.
Words and sounds fell out of my mouth like seeds.
I astonished myself.
My grandmother was like me exactly, only darker.

When I looked up, the black man had gone.
Only my own face startled me in the dark train window.

(from *Off Colour*, 1998)

Nigel Wheale

Nigel Wheale studied at Cambridge University under Jeremy Prynne in the early 1970s and taught at Cambridge College of Arts and Technology. The poet John Welch wrote of his work that 'it combines intellectual rigour and political awareness with a passionate commitment to lyric'.

Curlew Glide
Rises stuttering, a seeded trail of cries
flung between the green and the grey,
he marks his ground in song spraint.

At full curve from tail to beak tip,
wing blades flexed,
the arc of song
tense with an urgency we seem to know
thrills to a joyful alarm.

In the clearing of night
they are homeless star cries
stitched upon soft felt.

(from *Raw Skies*, 2006)

Lee Harwood

Lee Harwood's poetry stretches out from the mid-1960s when he was published by the innovative Fulcrum Press. The clarity and delicacy of much of his work earned him a reputation as one of the 'most resourceful and entertaining of contemporary British poets' (Peter Ackroyd). These two short pieces come from his most recently published work. The first poem refers to the collapsing Brighton pier, whilst the second has an almost Chinese quality of nearness and distance, presence and absence. Neither of them has a title.

> The old pier slumps into the sea after a winter storm. Wealthy residents collect the wreckage from the beach, planks they don't need. Battered bits of wood to sit with all those other oddments so proudly haggled for in the drizzle at a Sunday market.
>
> Dear Reader,
> Do you ever consider what age you will be when you die?
> and what will happen to your possessions?
> (from Take a card, Any card, 2003–2004)

> a grey sea a grey sky
> a seamless day with no hours
> flecks of snow on my coat
> family far away
> in foreign lands or waterlogged graves.
> (from Take a card, Any card, 2003–2004)

J.H. Prynne

J.H. Prynne has spent much of his life teaching English in Cambridge and his work has dominated the avant-garde world of poetry since the publication of *Kitchen Poems* in 1968. His second edition of *Poems*, a collection of chapbooks which concludes with the poem 'Blue Slides At Rest', was published in 2005. It was seen by Iain Sinclair as a collection in which the language is both astonishing and inevitable. The importance of Prynne's oeuvre was registered in Randall Stevenson's *Oxford English Literary History*. 'Refuse Collection' was printed in the online magazine *Quid*. This is an extract from the poem.

> ### Refuse Collection
> To a light led sole in pit of, this by slap-up
> barter of an arm rest cap, on stirrup trade in
> crawled to many bodies, uncounted. Talon up
> crude oil-for-food, incarnadine incarcerate, get

foremost a track rocket, rapacious in heavy
investment insert tool this way up. This way
can it will you they took to fast immediate satis-
faction or slather, new slave run the chain store
enlisted, posture writhing what they just want
we'll box tick that, nim nim. Camshot spoilers
trap to high stakes head to the ground elated
detonator like a bear dancing stripped canny
sex romp, webbing taint. Confess sell out the
self input, yes rape yes village gunship by
apache rotor capital genital grant a seed trial
take a nap a twin.

08.05.2004   (from IRA, Quid 13)

Peter Riley

Peter Riley has been publishing poetry since the 1960s. A review of his book-length
poem *Alstonefield* (2003) suggested that its 'considerable beauty' and 'intellectual
dexterity' deserved to find a larger readership. 'Introitus' refers to the time when
Riley was living on the south coast of England.

Introitus
How it begins:
                    it begins with me
walking along the shore at Hastings
just short of the surf line, on shingle.

To walk effectively on shingle you have to
lean forwards so you'd fall if you didn't push
your feet back from a firm step down and
back sharp forcing the separate ground
to consolidate underneath you, with a marked
flip as you lift each foot, scattering
stones behind, gaining momentum.

The shore's long and curves
slightly to the south as you approach the bar.
Winter; a hazy, cloudless day
and cold. No horizon to sea.

Looking up from this.
Stopping and raising the head,
correcting the stoop – a
small sea, its sound
on the stones, of the
wash back. Seagulls in winter

lose the harshness of their bark,
more a mewing, and there
aren't many.

It begins and either
stops there or doesn't.

That action, lifting the head,
the skin of the throat unfolding,
air reaching the upper chest
gazing out in no special direction –
position of receptiveness
each sense prepared to act; the body
hearkens – the mind is alerted.

That nothing comes
is good. No news
across the shore is
excellent, the truth
is there for a start.

The flesh is full
of what there is
there / then,
has that, offers
back self, is one
of all that.

And I lean again and
press the stones, bend
homeward, for the door
into what comes,
to bring it further.

(from *The Day's Final Balance*, 2007)

Anthony Barnett

Anthony Barnett's poems were originally collected in *The Resting Bell* (1987) produced by his own publishing firm, Allardyce, Barnett. *Miscanthus, Selected and New Poems* appeared in 2005. 'Stockholm, The Royal Library' concerns some of the work and artefacts belonging to Nelly Sachs, a German refugee poet who lived in Sweden from 1940. It was only after his visit to the Royal Library that Barnett realised he had no film in his camera. The prose piece 'The Carp' merges autobiography and history, as a frightened schoolboy visualises himself in a world that has echoes of the Gestapo.

Stockholm, The Royal Library
i.m. Nelly Sachs

I lift the dust from our books

A full circle drawn
from lake to harbour

Perched like a lamb on the terrace

Stork to take stock

Where is the ferry

Where did you talk

May I take photos

Uneasily

The flash eying your
                              carriage return

Eyid

Outside the Antiquarian

No film

Did not know

That

Reading

This

The counter reads

Zero

(from *Miscanthus*, 2005)

The Carp

He was travelling by train. The conductor's cap, rising and falling in steep peaks, jolted his memory of the officers' caps he recognised from the newsreels of his childhood or the features of adulthood. Perturbation. He sat in the compartment a half-century ago, more than that, before he was born, before the war was even begun, afraid in the pit of his stomach, in the corner of the playing field, waiting. Then it was over. He was transported along the same track, alone, with the

others, to the imaginary halt. He was not there, he
would never be there, he was never there, he was
pushing through a thicket, looking for his ticket, his
ticket, reflected in the glass.

(from Carp & Rubato, 1995)

John Welch

John Welch's poems explore the interrelation of personal inner-space and the outer
world of urban living. He wrote about his personal experience of breakdown and
psychoanalysis in an article 'Dream and Restoration' (in *Poets on Writing,* 1992).

Analysis

A mirror, it hung
In an empty house.
Being what there was
Between me and silence
Its monotonous glass
Was miles of nothing.
Approaching it
From one side, inching up carefully
Some tendrils of breath escaped me.
A tap gurgled. Sunlight paraded
Everywhere over a floor.
Statues hovered somewhere, the
Infuriating clouds
Were slowly moving off.
But what I am trying to remember is
How, swimming up towards me
Out of nowhere, once it
Borrowed my face for a moment.

Walking the endless streets since then
Where time and distance flow together
I lie in another town,
A different ceiling underneath my head.
The mirror's a plain man telling me.
He sits behind my shoulder.
His glass is harsh
         While I remember
How once I breathed, then wrote my name
On a blurred surface, solitary tracings.

(from The Eastern Boroughs, 2004)

4 | Critical approaches

- What do you understand by a poem having 'meaning'?

- How important is sound or music to the meaning of poetry?

- Where is the most helpful criticism to be found?

What does a poem mean?

The idea that words have simple meanings which can be deciphered was given a sharp shock in Lewis Carroll's *Through the Looking Glass and What Alice Found There*. Alice is confronted by the figure of Humpty Dumpty: having told her that 'un-birthday presents' are better than birthday presents, he says 'There's glory for you!' Understandably, Alice says that she doesn't know what he means by the word 'glory' and he replies 'Of course you don't – till I tell you. I meant *there's a nice knock-down argument for you!*':

> 'But *glory* doesn't mean 'a nice knock-down argument,' Alice objected.
> 'When *I* use a word,' Humpty Dumpty said in rather a scornful tone, 'it means just what I choose it to mean – neither more nor less.'
> 'The question is,' said Alice, 'whether you *can* make words mean different things.'
> 'The question is,' said Humpty Dumpty, 'which is to be master – that's all.'

There is of course a sinister sense here that words can mean whatever the 'master' in charge of a situation wishes them to mean. There is also a sense that if words are to be 'master', then they are more powerful than the person using them and we are trapped inside a language that has a definite and unchanging meaning.

It is worth bearing in mind one basic rule when you read contemporary poetry:

- Don't look for simple 'meanings': poetry isn't a riddle or a crossword puzzle which a reader is trying to solve.

In *Poetic Artifice* (1978), the poet and critic Veronica Forrest-Thomson referred to this crossword-puzzle approach to reading modern poetry when she objected to the tendency 'to make the already-known or already-thought the point of arrival', as if poetry were 'an obscure and figured statement which one understands by translating it into the already-known'. After all, why shouldn't we wait uncomfortably with the unfamiliar? Why should we assume automatically that a poem must have a 'meaning' that is just wrapped up in 'poetic language' that we need to unwrap in order to arrive at the sweet in the middle? Anthony Barnett's note on reading George Oppen seems an ideal place to start when contemplating some of the difficulties and surprises encountered in reading modern poetry:

> Reading an Oppen poem feels to me like setting out on a walk in the mountains. I am always turning unexpected bends and the objective in sight is always appearing, the same, but slightly different, from a different angle. You return either to the same spot by another route, but suddenly, unexpectedly, or you make the summit quickly and proceed quickly to the foot on another side. It simply affirms what we know of our politics and morality. A walk embarked on out of love. The poem and the walk restore. When you walk in the mountains, even an unfamiliar path, you know the basic geography. You have to be careful, when you wander lost, and while you think about the things you find in a George Oppen poem, think how careful George has been.
>
> (From *Paideuma*, Vol. 10, no. 1, Spring 1981; reprinted in *Carp & Rubato,* 1995)

Barnett's own poetry takes space very seriously indeed, making the whiteness of the page articulate (see Introduction, page 8). What becomes increasingly evident is the importance of the nature of selection and the concentration upon individual words as 'things', placed pebble by pebble on the page. In an essay on Barnett's poetry (1992), Michael Grant suggested that 'the value of a poem' was closely linked to 'its making present the processes of selection out of which it has been produced':

> To engage with the significance of a poem is to engage with the ways in which it could have been other than it is.

Sound and meaning

The French critic Julia Kristeva identified the power of sound patterns in poetry which disrupt the linear development of thought. She suggested that the haunting quality of poetry is bound up with sound effects, also pointed out by Catherine Belsey:

> These sound effects, as they reappear in poetry, are musical, patterned; they disrupt the purely 'thetic' (thesis-making) logic of rational argument by drawing on a sense or sensation that Kristeva locates beyond surface meaning.
>
> (*Poststructuralism, a very short introduction*, 2002)

A fine example of how the sound of a piece of poetry can convey its meaning is the anonymous late-medieval lyric, 'Western Wind' (see Part 2, page 54):

Western wind when wilt thou blow
The small rain down can rain –
Christ, if my love were in my arms
And I in my bed again.

The sense of loss is conveyed not only by the juxtaposition of the alliterative use of 'w' in the opening line with the diminutive ordinariness of 'small rain', but also by the emphatic 'Christ' at the beginning of the third line. There is a sound of desperation in the emphasis which brings to mind the loss of the beloved and the quality of her importance contained in the simplicity of the reference to 'bed again'. The value of the memory is contained in such a simple location and in the echoing sound of the last word which stretches beyond the limit of the poem.

L=A=N=G=U=A=G=E poetry

One interesting spin-off from this debate about meaning is the American-based L=A=N=G=U=A=G=E school of poetry. In this poetry the assumed place of a speaker, a person, in a poem is challenged and value is accorded to words as entities or objects. One of the most useful discussions of this type of writing can be found in *Ideas of Space in Contemporary Poetry* by Ian Davidson (2007). In the chapter 'Aesthetics of Space: Cubism to Language Poetry' he suggests that in L=A=N=G=U=A=G=E poetry the history of a particular word, along with its so-called 'authentic' meaning that can be traced back through a dictionary and through patterns of language usage, does not prevent its meaning from being replaced as the context changes. Meanings become dependent upon the user of the word:

The language poets set out to explore this relationship, and the way that the meanings of words are contextually derived from their place in the language system rather than from their correspondence with a 'real' or 'concrete' world.

In this book Davidson explores the impact of ideas of space and collage on contemporary poetry; and discusses poets who are trying to deal with the complexities of a post-modern world and who are 'unwilling to reduce experience to the neatly turned lyric'. He also examines the world of the relationship between the Internet, digital technologies and the art of the poet.

Another important essay to consult on the issue of meanings is Marjorie Perloff's 'The Word as Such' (republished in *The Dance of the Intellect*, 1996) where she highlights the prominent role in this field of writing played by the

English poet Tom Raworth. Raworth's poetry allows the reader an active role in the creation of possible meanings. David Caddy noted the fun and unpredictable nature of this writing in his review of the poems:

> The reader is made to think differently through the use of collage, surrealistic juxtapositions and an inventive playfulness. His poetry is as unpredictable as Spike Milligan in full flow. From Olson's open-field poetics he derived the sense that a poem can draw upon any source. He added a child-like word play.
>
> (from *The Use of English*, Autumn 2003)

In 'thoughts are in real time' (1993) Raworth has a sense of fast-moving interaction:

> thoughts are in real time
> after you've gone
> they keep your body alive
> sending bills
> bankrupting
> your children
> reserving the right
> to legally define
> alive
> perhaps
> that technological blip
> records decay
> evening sunlight
> first sense of spring

As Caddy points out:

> The reader need not be over-worried about the location of meaning within the contents of a particular poem. It is perhaps more a matter of assessing the balance, the suitability of the music for the contents assembled. Meaning, as such, is in the process of reading, in the journey, the associations and connections that the words and sequence of words create for the individual reader.

This poetry of performance is captured on *Rock Drill,* part of a series of readings by contemporary poets on CD. Interestingly, the quiet and meditative tones of Lee Harwood are also available in this series. Andrea Brady's *Archive of the Now* website from Brunel University contains an eclectic range of poets and poems, including J.H. Prynne reading 'Cocaine' by the American Boston poet, John Wieners. Keith Tuma comments on Raworth as performer of his own work:

As a performer, Raworth is known for the speed of his delivery, which is tailored to the modular shape and mercurial movement of his poems.

(Introduction to *Anthology of Twentieth-Century British and Irish Poetry*, 2001)

In 1972 Raworth had mentioned that he had no 'sense of questing for knowledge' in the sense that Charles Olson had, but instead 'My idea is to go the other way, you know. And to be completely empty and then see what sounds.' ('An Exhibition', *Cambridge Conference on Contemporary Poetry 8*, 1998)

Some important books of criticism

In addition to the many critical references which can be found throughout this book, there are some particular texts which are of significant importance.

The Last of England? by Randall Stevenson (*The Oxford English Literary History* Volume 12: 1960–2000, 2005)

In this major survey of literature of the last forty years of the 20th century, Stevenson suggests that language disruption and challenges to literary convention feature widely in the world of poetry. In a central chapter on 'Politics and Postmodernism' he compares the anthology world of Bloodaxe's *The New Poetry* (1993) with Iain Sinclair's *Conductors of Chaos* (1996). The former was noted for its inclusion of poets such as Sean O'Brien, Simon Armitage and Jo Shapcott and for its editors' assertion that the new generation of poets of the 1990s were distinguished by 'accessibility, democracy and responsiveness'. They reaffirmed the significance of poetry as 'public utterance'. By contrast, in his Introduction Sinclair was sceptical about 'public utterance' and included poems which were more fully engaged with 'the complexity of the climate in which they exist'. In the introductory comments to the selection of J.H. Prynne's work in *Conductors of Chaos*, the poet Ian Patterson wrote that the poems were 'in a sense, photographs of processes of thought, catching the instant on the wing and flying with it'. Prynne's 'Afterword to Original: Chinese Language-Poetry Group' opens with the now-famous comment 'Within the great aquarium of language the light refracts variously and can bounce by inclinations not previously observed.' As Randall Stevenson points out, Prynne's poetry seems to be involved with the processes at work within language; in a later chapter he quotes from Donald Davie's poem, 'Essex', where the poet suggested that 'names and things named don't match' and 'sooner or later the whole / Cloth of the language peels off / As wallpaper peels from a wall'.

***Poets on Writing* edited by Denise Riley (1992)**
The thirty-six essays and poems that make up this volume cover a vast range
of subjects and approaches, from the world of 'Small-Press Publication' (Nigel
Wheale) to 'The State of Poetry Today' (Tom Raworth). Michael Haslam's essay on
'The Subject of Poems' unashamedly asserts that 'poetry is a quest for truth, and
purity, and essence' whilst Carlyle Reedy's 'Working Processes of a Woman Poet'
says that 'the working processes of poetry include inspiration / motivation, material
/ language used, and image / sound consequent upon language'.

***Contemporary British Poetry, Essays in Theory and Criticism*, edited by
James Acheson and Romana Huk (1996)**
In addition to the essay on 'Black Men's Poetry in Britain' by Alistair Niven (see Part
2, page 61), this collection includes a range of writing, from specific work on Carol
Ann Duffy and Roy Fisher to 'Poetry and the Women's Movement' and 'From the
Lost Ground: Liz Lochhead, Douglas Dunn and Contemporary Scottish Poetry'. In
the introduction, Romana Huk suggests that 'the current poetry scene in Britain
demands renewed attention from readers and critics alike because … it is richly
enacting the breakdown of older orders'.

***Other: British and Irish Poetry since 1970* by Richard Caddel and Peter
Quartermain (1999)**
The full introduction to this anthology of poetry is available on the Internet in
Jacket # 4. This provides an excellent introduction to the ideas of modernism and
mainstream in contemporary poetry. It opens with a reference to the Middle Ages of
William Langland's *Piers the Ploughman*:

> The British Isles have long been, self-evidently, crowded, complex,
> and packed with chaotic overlays of cultures – local, imported
> or created – which develop and intermix constantly. Langland's
> 14th-century 'fair field full of folk' was already an intensely plural
> society, where elements of Saxon, Norman and Cymric were evident
> alongside each other, with strong elements of Latinate church
> culture, and, never far away, mainland European culture jostling
> alongside the other elements of linguistic mix. Diverse cultures
> sometimes conflict violently, or sometimes make uneasy alliances,
> and sometimes, perhaps by chance, give rise to the creation of new
> forms or achievements.

***Distant reading: Performance, Readership, and Consumption in
Contemporary Poetry* by Peter Middleton (2005)**
The chapter on reading poetry in the 1990s, 'The New Memoryism', opens with a
perspective on the decade:

When I perform an act of introspection and try to find memories of the nineties, all I find are disordered news images and traces of personal memory: incinerated Iraqis outside Kuwait City; John Major's grin and Bill Clinton's grin and hugs; my children in different sizes and degrees of emotional command; or a computer that has just lost what I was writing. Are those years themselves already lost, the engrams too faint, just a vast scrap heap of sensed moments, tags of speech, comings and goings, passions and research exercises, pages and tele-news-websites of faded insights?

Middleton refers to the mobile phone, the Internet, the personal computer and digital image processing as having an enormous impact upon the way we live; he registers that they 'are genetically modifying the ways we remember and the ways we read'. Middleton refers to Prynne's poem number 7 in *For the Monogram* (1997) as making 'the new communications technology part of their field of reference, semantic, visual, and lexical, all broadly at the level of content':

> Select an object with no predecessors. Clip off its
> roots, reset to zero and remove its arrows. At each
> repeat decrement the loop to an update count for all
> successors of the removed object ranking the loop body
> at next successor to the array stack.

Assignments

1 Which of the critics or critical approaches discussed above have done most to increase your understanding of how to respond to modern poetry?

2 Is it more important to start with the sound or the meaning of a poem? Illustrate your argument by analysing the impact of one or more of the poems in Part 3 in the light of the comments made by any of the critics discussed.

3 'Diverse cultures sometimes conflict violently, or sometimes make uneasy alliances, and sometimes, perhaps by chance, give rise to the creation of new forms or achievements.' (Caddel and Quartermain) How accurately does this describe the development of modern poetry as illustrated in this book?

5 | How to write about contemporary poetry

- What are the central issues in contemporary poetry?
- How do poems allow the 'unseen' to become 'seen'?

Close reading

In *52 Ways of looking at a Poem*, Ruth Padel suggests that one of the purposes of poetry is 'to transform real life imaginatively, so we understand our lives new-paintedly, more fully'. When you read a poem that might appear initially both new and difficult, it is important to remember that poets do not write to be read by either critics or by examination students. They write because they want to be read by people who will both enjoy the newness of the vision of life offered, and recognise something more of their own life by reflection.

The themes which have long dominated Western art are as much present in the world of Seamus Heaney, Charles Tomlinson, Tony Harrison or Vicki Feaver, as they were in the worlds of Aeschylus, Shakespeare, Dante or Wordsworth: the transience of human life, power and political motivation, the relationship of parent to child and child to parent, sorrow, loss, beauty, joy, love, guilt, envy, hatred, fear and sometimes sheer wonder. Perhaps the central thing to remember when writing about contemporary poetry is the vital nature of close textual analysis. Meanings are intimately and irrevocably bound up with words, the way they are used, the way they sound; and words are used in patterned form in poetry, whether in rhyming or in spaced clarity across a page. It is necessary to be aware of some of the central devices of patterning, such as imagery, metaphor, metre, and stanza.

'Yews': a brief analysis

An example of how you might approach close textual analysis is this brief analysis of Vicki Feaver's short poem, 'Yews' (Part 3, page 66). Since it is important to see how poems can be compared, read it alongside Carol Ann Duffy's 'Demeter' (Part 3, page 67).

A yew tree is a dark-wood, coniferous tree that has dark foliage and red berries; it is often planted in churchyards and associated with mourning; the wood of the tree was traditionally used for making bows. Apart from the fleshy part of the red berries, the tree is poisonous and this is especially true of the needles. In England, the Celts used the area surrounding a yew tree as a burial ground and the trees themselves may have been seen as gateways to the land of the dead. It is quite possible that when Christianity was first brought to the country, churches were built around yew trees as a way of bringing together the two religious cultures.

The opening lines of the poem evoke a sense of the long-gone past with the word 'Vikings', and their bloodthirsty and invasive reputation is suggested by the idea of their spilled blood feeding the poisonous tree which now stands. The yew is 'Fed on' their blood and the idea of battle is given a visual sense with the word 'stained'. As the poet continues the image of growth she sees the trees as being 'driven' out of the earth, and the passionate nature of their bloody origins will now 'break out' in the poisonous 'feathery needles'. The use of the botanical terms, 'xylem' and 'phloem', the harder and softer parts of the fibro-vascular tissue (the wood), promotes the feeling that the ancient world is very much alive in the modern: Vikings in the world of scientific names.

The tree itself is associated with emotions, and 'passions' which 'break out' are aspects of human behaviour. This sense of the tree being alive is further emphasised by the personification of branches 'twisting into necks', bringing to mind the sort of picture that might well be found in Gustave Doré's illustration to Canto XIII of Dante's *Inferno* where the souls of suicides have been transformed into living trees. As well as the 'venom in feathery needles', poison can be found in the seeds lying within the attractive red berries, and Feaver seems to delight in a sense of female revenge in the idea of destruction being associated with the softness of 'pulp / of the female's orange berries'. At this point, with the tree standing before us, the poet places herself firmly within its aura, standing beneath the sweeping downward movement of the branches. As she stands 'in their smothering tents' she seems to be imprisoned in a place 'where nothing grows'. The density of the dark branches and the evergreen needles ensure that the ground surrounding the tree gets little light – this emphasises the idea of a cell, as the poet stands there 'adjusting to the thin light'. From within her prison, the poet seems to relax, unwind, and be drawn to

> the sleepiness of thinking
> this would be the moment
> to lie down and die.

One point of view is that this is a firmly feminist poem where the trapped female, the imprisoned woman, can only wreak her revenge on the male prisoner through her children, 'seeds buried in the pulp', who will themselves burst up through the earth, carrying her spleen into the next generation. However, another view argues that there is a deeply moving sense of the queen at the centre of her mystical world, standing in the tents with a drowsy sense of what Keats referred to as being 'half in love with easeful Death' ('Ode to a Nightingale').

A comparison with 'Demeter'

The narrator of this poem contrasts strongly with that of 'Yews' in the way that the bereaved mother awaits the return of her lost daughter, Persephone. She too feels imprisoned in her isolation and her dwelling place is 'winter and hard earth'. In contrast with the sheltering imprisonment of the 'smothering tents' of branches, Demeter sits alone 'in my cold stone room', where the wintry absence of love is caught with her choice of words, 'tough words, granite, flint'. In her seasonal isolation she tries to 'break the ice' as an attempt to thaw out of loneliness into a world of new hope. Her unhappiness is emphasised by the starkly simple phrase, 'My broken heart', which has become like a stone. When she tries to look outwards from the imprisoning loneliness her heart 'skimmed, / flat, over the frozen lake.' However, unlike the dream-like resignation into the world of 'resinous stillness' felt by the narrator of 'Yews', here Demeter's openness to love, her hope for change, is rewarded by the distant but approaching resurrection of her daughter, returning from the underworld in which she has been trapped for the winter:

> She came from a long, long way,
> but I saw her at last, walking,
> my daughter, my girl, across the fields

The yearning expectation is expressed by the repetition of 'long' and the way that 'daughter' becomes 'girl' as she comes closer into focus 'across the fields'. The delight in the recognition of a restored child is emphasised by the ordinariness of the image in the following line, where the girl appears 'in bare feet' as though she too has suffered an imprisonment like her mother in a world of barrenness. As 'winter', 'hard earth', 'cold stone room', 'granite', 'flint' thaw into reconciliation and expressed love, the eyewitness account moves in its simplicity:

> I swear
> the air softened and warmed as she moved

The conclusion, so different from the imprisonment of revenge and poison, is beautifully contained with the domestic vision of childhood's delight:

> the blue sky smiling, none too soon,
> with the small shy mouth of a new moon.

Exploring comparisons

A further interesting comparison can be made with Tomlinson's 'In a Cambridge Garden' (Part 3, page 79) where the importance of a meeting and a parting dominate the quietness of the scene. In discussing the relative importance of 'place', where one lives, Tomlinson concludes that there is some portion of the world to which an individual feels inextricably bound. The English poet, Tomlinson, feels bound to the land where he thought that he could teach his countrymen 'to see / The changing English light':

> like water
> That drips off a gunwale driving through the sea,
> Showing the way the whole world
> Dipping through space and cloud and sun,
> Surges across the day as it travels on
> Turning.

The painterly vision of movement and the effects of light on water could be contrasted with the sparse monosyllabic world that surrounds Demeter as she 'sat in my cold stone room'. 'Demeter' highlights a mythical figure who has lost her daughter to the underworld for a part of the year; Tomlinson's poem has a personal reference to a close friend, Octavio Paz. However, one doesn't need to know the exact reference here in order to register the thought and emotion of what is being expressed. In the second of Peter Robinson's interviews, he says that 'poems need to stand relatively alone':

> If the reader cannot tell who I'm talking to or why … then suffice to say that I don't think the reader needs to know.

Robinson goes on to refer to formal Japanese gardens where there is a bamboo device that sends a drop of water into a pond at intervals to emphasise silence. The 17th-century Japanese haiku writer, Basho, wrote three lines that have become world-famous:

furu ike ya	old pond:
kawazu tobikomu	a frog jumps in
mizu no oto	sound of water

Horikiri Minoru's account of these lines says that the focus of the verse is without question the 'sound of water':

> Generally *mizu no oto* (sound of water) means the sound of flowing or dripping water, but because in this verse it is the tiny sound made when a frog jumps into water, it expresses limitless silence all the more.
>
> (from *Poetic Spaces*, 2006)

He goes on to recount how, at a conference discussing haiku, one of the contributing scholars suggested that, due to their streamlined shape, frogs do not in fact make a noise when jumping into water:

> One might say that the sound of water that Basho heard was not one audible to the ear, but one that was audible to the mind.

However, myths tell us who we are. The poet Robert Duncan, a friend and colleague of Charles Olson at Black Mountain College, refers to a sense of 'universal humanity' which is to be discovered in 'the mixing-ground of man's commonality in myth':

> The meaning and intent of what it is to be a man and, among men, to be a poet, I owe to the workings of myth in my spirit, both the increment of associations gathered in my continuing study of mythological lore and my own apprehension of what my life is at work there. The earliest stories heard, nursery rimes and animal tales from childhood, remain today alive in my apprehensions, for there is a ground of man's imaginations of what he is in which my own nature as a man is planted and grows.
>
> (from *The Truth & Life of Myth*, 1968)

Duncan recalls looking at pictures with his sister, 'my mother between us'. The picture that he remembers is of three young men sleeping on a mat, one of whom is Basho, the 17th-century Japanese writer of haiku. Basho has just woken up – the poem of the frog jumping into an ancient pond echoes down the years. The preoccupations of the Japanese poet resonate with contemporary poets: the importance of syllables, words as single thoughts, taking moments one by one. The most important way of writing about contemporary poetry is to concentrate upon those echoing sounds and meanings which allow the 'unseen' ideas and feelings to become the 'seen': poets write poems so that they can share what they think and feel.

Assignments

1   In a reading of the two poems below by Andrew Motion and Geoff Ward is it possible to argue that one is more straightforward than the other? Does the metaphor of Motion's 'A Wall' reveal a more direct 'meaning' than the world opened up by Ward's 'Distance Learning'? Does a comparison of the two, and in particular of the contexts in which each was published (see note below), suggest anything about the difference between types of contemporary poetry?

A Wall
I have forgotten whatever
it was I wanted to say,
also the way I wanted
to say it. Form and music.

I should just look at the things
that are, and fix myself
to the earth. This wall,
facing me over the street,

smooth as a shaven chin
but pocked with holes
that scaffolders left,
and flicked with an over-

flow flag. Which still
leaves pigeon-shit,
rain-streaks, washing.
Or maybe it's really

a board where tiny
singing meteors strike?
I rest my case. I rest
my case and cannot imagine

hunger greater than this.
For marks.
For messages sent by hand.
For signs of life

Distance Learning

He seemed to have been walking forever
Up the green lane, along the narrow lane
He seemed to have been walking forever

Along the green lane where it twisted and looped
He came at last to a pane of glass
The size of a mousehole in a house that sighed
And quivered, as he stooped

To look inside. And there, in a bare sunlit
Room hardly larger than your hand
Stood, gravely, a rook
Who raised reluctantly one stygian velvet wing

And there between the feathers gleamed
The gold band of a ring.
Inside the ring there ran an endless corridor
Of blue, and at its end, a zigzag flue.

He climbed in, fell through space then found
Himself at last on a revolving stage
Bare, except for where a spotlight fell
On a single rose. He sped through the heart

Until he reached its smouldering, cold core
And there amid the breath of rustling ashes found
A door, then another, when suddenly
He thought he could smell the sea

And there fell from the air a silver shell
With a folded scroll inside,
Which he unrolled, and on which he found written
In a graceful and oddly familiar hand,

Protect your clothes from exploiting you.

Note: Andrew Motion's *Selected Poems 1976–1997* is published by Faber &
Faber, the publishing firm which had T.S. Eliot on its editorial board and was
the main promoter of Ted Hughes – Motion's predecessor as Poet Laureate.
'A Wall' comes from Motion's volume *Public Property* which Faber published
in 2003 and is included in *New British Poetry*. By contrast, Geoff Ward has
published six collections of poems with Causeway Press, Infernal Methods,
Window Books including *Mondegreen* (Equipage, Cambridge, 2000).
'Distance Learning' is anthologised in *Vanishing Points*.

2   Look closely at the language of Tony Harrison's *A Cold Coming* and
    Robert Minhinnick's 'The Tooth' (Part 3, pages 86 and 92). Both
    poems deal with the devastation and horror of war in the Middle East,
    but approach the topic in very different ways. Which do you find more
    effective, more moving? Compare the language of outrage in both and, by
    close reference to the texts, analyse the methods used by the two poets to
    awaken the reader's consciousness to the plight of ordinary people caught
    up in political and national disasters.

3   Compare the following two poems in terms of their language and
    imagery. Can they be read without involving a simple search for
    'meaning'? The first is by Selima Hill; the second by Peter Didsbury.

A Small Hotel
My nipples tick
like little bombs of blood.

Someone is walking
in the yard outside.

I don't know why
Our Lord was crucified.

A really good fuck
makes me feel like custard.

The Shorter Life
I loved the rain,
but always suffered badly
from post-pluvial *tristesse*.

My best wet afternoon was in the mouth
of a disused railway tunnel,
behind me the mile-long carbon-encrusted dark.

6 | Resources

Books about poetry

Donald Davie *Thomas Hardy and British Poetry* (Oxford University Press, 1972)

Peter Robinson *Talk about Poetry, Conversations on the Art* (Shearsman Books, 2006)

Ralph Maud, ed. *Charles Olson Reader* (Carcanet, 2005)

Ruth Padel *The Poem and the Journey* (Chatto and Windus, 2007)

Poetry anthologies

Neil Astley, ed. *New Blood* (Bloodaxe, 1999)

Richard Caddel and Peter Quartermain, ed. *Other: British and Irish Poetry since 1970* (Wesleyan University Press, 1999)

Michael Horovitz, ed. *Grandchildren of Albion* (New Departures, 1992)

Michael Hulse, David Kennedy and David Morley, eds. *The New Poetry* (Bloodaxe, 1993)

Rod Mengham and John Kinsella, eds. *Vanishing Points* (Salt, 2004)

Don Paterson and Charles Simic, eds. *New British Poetry* (Graywolf Press, 2004)

Deryn Rees-Jones, ed. *Modern Women Poets* (Bloodaxe, 2005)

Jerome Rothenberg and Pierre Joris, eds. *Poems for the Millennium* (University of California, 1995)

Carol Rumens, ed. *New Women Poets* (Bloodaxe, 1990)

Iain Sinclair, ed. *Conductors of Chaos* (Picador, 1996)

Keith Tuma, ed. *Anthology of Twentieth-Century British and Irish Poetry* (Oxford University Press, 2001)

Poetry presses and websites

As this book has stressed, some of the most exciting new poetry is being published not by the commercial publishing houses but by small presses. These presses are run by enthusiasts, often practising poets themselves, and many of them also sponsor or promote poetry readings, conferences and magazines – online as well as hard copy. A good sense of who is making the news in contemporary poetry can therefore be gained by visiting the websites of some of these presses, identifying their particular slant on poetry, noting which poets they most actively promote and assessing the range of their activities. Some of the websites post freely downloadable back-numbers of magazines in which you can read reviews and articles about poets who are challenging and changing public attitudes to poetry. It is striking that, almost without exception, the presses listed below are located outside London.

Barque   www.barquepress.com
Barque publishes chapbooks and full-length poetry collections as well as CD-Roms and the magazine *Quid*.

Bloodaxe   www.bloodaxebooks.com
Bloodaxe Books, founded in 1978 and based in Newcastle, has a website that offers information about all the very wide range of poets (past and present) whom it publishes. In addition, its webpage 'New to Poetry' (www.bloodaxebooks.com/newto.asp) offers valuable links to many of the writers and topics introduced in the earlier parts of this book

Carcanet   www.carcanet.co.uk
Carcanet, founded by the poet and critic Michael Schmidt, is based, like Bloodaxe, well away from London, in Manchester. Its webpages feature reviews and useful articles devoted to its poets, many of whom are award-winning writers, while others stand well away from the mainstream. Carcanet also publishes the leading poetry journal, *PN Review*.

Equipage   www.cambridgepoetry.org
Equipage is a publisher firmly located in Cambridge: it is part of *Cambridgepoetry*, an umbrella organisation centred on the University's English Faculty, which organises readings, conferences and festivals, bringing together many of the key figures in contemporary poetry. It has a strong interest in poetry in translation.

Etruscan   www.e-truscan.co.uk
A Devon-based publisher, whose individual books of poems by individual authors such as Ian Sinclair and Tom Pickard, are complemented by the Etruscan Readers series, which introduces three contemporary poets in each volume.

Flambard   www.flambardpress.co.uk

Flambard Press specialises in bringing the work of young and relatively unknown writers to a wider audience. At the same time, it publishes the poetry of major figures from other genres – for example, the playwright Arnold Wesker.

Litter   www.leafepress.com

Litter is a free online magazine of contemporary poetry, combining new writing, reviews, essays and interviews. Published by the Leafe Press, it is edited by Alan Baker, whose 'Editor's Blog' offers some valuable and accessible insights into the problems of writing, reading and publishing poetry today.

Salt   www.saltpublishing.com

Salt Publishing has a strong commitment to international writers, not surprising for an enterprise whose roots are in both Australia *and* Cambridge. Its website provides useful biographies of its authors. It also supplies extracts from some of its recent titles to give readers a clear sense of the range of poetry that Salt promotes.

Shearsman   www.shearsman.com

Shearsman and *Shearsman* magazine have been edited in Exeter by Tony Frazer since 1981. His taste is wide, as he explains on his Editor's Page: 'In terms of the magazine's position with regard to contemporary poetry, there is a clear inclination towards the more exploratory end of the current spectrum. Notwithstanding this, however, quality work of a more conservative kind will always be considered seriously … I tend to like mixing work from both ends of the spectrum in the magazine, and firmly believe that good writing can, and should, cohabit with other forms of good writing, regardless of the aesthetic that drives it.' Some of the Shearsman e-books are freely downloadable from the Shearsman website.

Shoestring   www.shoestringpress.co.uk

Based in Nottingham, the Shoestring Press says about itself: 'We specialise in sequences as well as collections by (usually) established but unfashionable poets or poets whom we are introducing to British readers for the first time, even though they may be well known elsewhere.'

Smith / Doorstep   www.poetrybusiness.co.uk

The Poetry Business, located in Sheffield, publishes collections of poetry under its Smith / Doorstep imprint, runs workshops for writers and publishes the well-esteemed poetry journal, *The North*. The Poetry Business also produces recordings of poets such as Carol Ann Duffy and Simon Armitage, reading and discussing their work.

Worple Press   www.worplepress.com
Founded in 1997 by the poet Peter Carpenter and his wife Amanda in Tonbridge, the Worple Press has a small but distinguished list of poets, including Ian Sinclair, Elizabeth Cook and Clive Wilmer.

Other poetry websites

The Argotist   www.argotistonline.co.uk
The *Argotist Online* 'publishes non-mainstream poetry, and features essays and interviews related to it'. As the editor, Jeffrey Side, explains, 'By non-mainstream, I mean poetry that is aware of the plasticity of language and which places connotation and ambiguity over denotation and precision of meaning. This sort of poetry invites interpretation and allows for plurality of meaning as opposed to hermeneutic closure.' This online magazine allows free access to a valuable collection of articles, interviews and contemporary poetry.

Jacket   www.jacketmagazine.com
An interesting and comprehensive Australian online poetry journal. Among its most useful and unusual features are discussions of recent volumes of poetry, featuring interviews with the authors and notes providing context for the poems.

Magma   www.magmapoetry.com
Published in hard copy, but back numbers and key articles and interviews are available online. No single editor: each issue is edited by a group of contributors.

Nthposition   www.nthposition.com
An online journal that ranges across politics, poetry and fiction. One of its best pages provides links to a wide variety of further poetry resources.

Penned in the Margins   www.pennedinthemargins.co.uk
Penned in the Margins helpfully combines an up-to-date blog, listing (mostly London-based) poetry events with reviews and news, plus links to a number of otherwise obscure poetry websites.

Poetry Society   www.poetrysociety.org.uk
The Poetry Society's website is valuable not only for the links it provides to a host of different poetry sites and organisations, mainstream and otherwise, but particularly for its monthly podcasts which provide access to poets taking about themselves and each other, especially about their debts to other writers

Tears in the Fence   www.myspace.com/tearsinthefence
A 144-page book of poetry, prose poems, fiction, essays, translations, interviews and reviews published three times a year. Edited by David Caddy.

Poets' websites

An increasing number of poets have their own websites. Here are some belonging to writers featured elsewhere in this book.

David Caddy	www.davidcaddy.blogspot.com
Michael Haslam	www.continualesong.com
Tom Raworth	www.tomraworth.com
Todd Swift	www.toddswift.com
Peter Riley	www.aprileye.co.uk

Glossary

Chapbooks small, paper-covered booklets, usually printed on a single sheet or portion of a sheet, folded into books of eight, twelve, sixteen and twenty-four pages.

Closed/fixed form poetry which has an established pattern such as the haiku, a three-line poem with a set syllable pattern of 5-7-5, or the sonnet with fourteen lines.

Collage a work of art in which cut-out pieces of photographs, printed pictures or other items are used together to build an image.

Dramatic monologue a type of poem in which a character, often a historical figure, delivers a speech explaining his or her own feelings. This style of poetry was made particularly famous by the Victorian poet, Robert Browning. He created 'dramatic monologues' for Renaissance characters so that they could reveal the motives for their actions ('My Last Duchess', 'Andreo del Sarto', 'Fra Lippo Lippi').

Hermeneutic the art or science of interpretation of meaning.

Intertextuality the shaping of a text's meanings by reference to other texts. This can involve an author's borrowing and transformation of a prior text, or can refer to a reader's recognising a reference being carried over from one text to another.

Metaphysical studying the first principles of things, such as 'being', 'time', 'identity'.

Open form poetry which does not have an established pattern to it, whether it be in line length, metre, rhyme, imagery, syntax, or stanzas.

Reductive capable of being reduced to a simple answer.

Index

Acknowledgements

The authors and publishers acknowledge the following sources of copyright material and are grateful for the permissions granted. While every effort has been made, it has not always been possible to identify the sources of all the material used, or to trace all copyright holders. If any omissions are brought to our notice, we will be happy to include the appropriate acknowledgements on reprinting.

pp.32–3: The Argotist for an extract by Tony Frazer from *The Argotist Online*; pp.103, 106, 103: Anthony Barnett for 'Stockholm, The Royal Library' from *Miscanthus: Selected and New Poems* by Anthony Barnett, Shearsman (2005). Copyright © Anthony Barnett 2005; 'A Note About George Oppen', *Paideuma*, 10:1 (1981), revised as 'Note Through a Lens' from *Carp and Rubato* by Anthony Barnett, Invisible Books (1995). Copyright © Anthony Barnett 1981; and 'The Carp' from *Carp and Rubato* by Anthony Barnett, Invisible Books (1995). Copyright © Anthony Barnett 1995; pp.97, 75, 93, 94: Bloodaxe Books for Jackie Kay 'Pride' from *Darling: New and Selected Poems* by Jackie Kay (2007); Barry MacSweeney 'Pearl's Utter Brilliance' and 'Pearl Alone' from *Wolf Tongue* (2003); Roy Fisher 'They Come Home' and 'Going' from *The Long and the Short of It* (2005); p.85: David Caddy for 'The Atmosphere' from *The Willy Poems* (2004); pp.7, 79, 83, 92, 108, 14: Carcanet Press Ltd for Charles Tomlinson 'Aesthetic' and 'In a Cambridge Garden' from *Door in the Wall* by Charles Tomlinson (1992); R.F. Langley 'Man Jack' from *Collected Poems* by R.F. Langley (2000); and extracts from Robert Minhinnick 'The Tooth' from *King Driftwood* by Robert Minhinnick (2008) and Tom Raworth 'Thoughts Are in Real Time' in 'Eternal Section' from *Collected Poems* by Tom Raworth (1994); and with New Directions Publishing Corp. for William Carlos Williams 'The Red Wheel Barrow' from *The Collected Poems: Volume 1, 1909–1939* by William Carlos Williams. Copyright © 1938 by New Directions Publishing Corp.; p.8: Columbia University for William Bronk 'Her Singing' from *Life Supports: New and Collected Poems* by William Bronk. Copyright © The Trustees of Columbia University in the City of New York; p.74: Jean Crozier for Andrew Crozier 'Blank Misgivings' from *Vanishing Points* (2004); p.62: Curtis Brown Group Ltd on behalf of the author for Grace Nichols 'Epilogue' from *I is a Long Memoried Woman* by Grace Nichols. Copyright © Grace Nichols 1983; p.56: Dedalus Press for Pat Boran 'A Natural History of Armed Conflict' from *New and Selected Poems* by Pat Boran (2007); pp.23, 52, 72, 70, 81: Faber & Faber Ltd for Douglas Dunn 'Home Again' from *Elegies* (1985); with Random House Inc for an extract from W.H. Auden 'September 1, 1939' from *Collected Poems* by W.H. Auden. Copyright © 1940, renewed 1968, by W.H. Auden; and with Farrar, Straus and Giroux, LLC for Seamus Heaney 'District and Circle' from *District and Circle* by Seamus Heaney. Copyright © 2006 by Seamus Heaney, Seamus Heaney 'The Crossing' from 'Inferno: Canto III' from *Seeing Things* by Seamus Heaney. Copyright © 1991 by Seamus Heaney; and Ted Hughes 'Visit' from *Birthday Letters* by Ted Hughes. Copyright © 1998 by Ted Hughes; p.86: Tony Harrison for 'A Cold Coming' from *A Cold Coming* by Tony Harrison, Bloodaxe Books (1991); p.96: David Higham Associates on behalf of the author for Fred D'Aguiar 'Home' from *British Subjects* by Fred Aguiar, Bloodaxe Books (1993); p.100: Lee Harwood for 'The old pier slumps …' and 'a grey sea a grey sky …' from *Collected Poems, 1964–2004* by Lee Harwood, Shearsman Books (2004); p.76: Lilian MacSweeney for Barry MacSweeney 'I Looked Down on a Child Today' from *Wolf Tongue* (2003); p.30: Peter Makin for an extract from *Shearsman*, 69:70, Autumn 2006/Winter 2007; p.34: New Statesman for an extract from Neil Astley 'Give Poetry Back to People', *New Statesman*, 23.10.06; p.100: J.H. Prynne for 'Refuse Collection' included in *Quid*, 13 (2004); pp.65, 66: The Random House Group Ltd for Vicki Feaver 'Judith' from *The Handless Maiden* by Vicki Feaver, Jonathan Cape (1994); and Vicki Feaver 'Yews' from *The Book of Blood* by Vicki Feaver, Jonathan Cape (2006); p.101: Peter Riley for 'Introitus' from *The Day's Final Balance* by Peter Riley (2007); pp.66, 67, 68, 50, 42: Rogers, Coleridge and White Ltd on behalf of the authors for Carol Ann Duffy 'Little Red-Cap', 'Demeter', 'If I Was Dead' and an extract from 'Salome'. Copyright © Carol Ann Duffy 2007; and an extract by Don Paterson from an article in *Guardian Review*, 6.11.04, pp.34–5; p.69: Carol Rumens for 'Poem: From a Conversation during Divorce' from *Best China Sky* by Carol Rumens, Bloodaxe Books (1997); p.59: Sunday Tribune for an extract from an article by Seamus Heaney, *Sunday Tribune*, September (1994); p.104: John Welch for 'Analysis from The Eastern Boroughs (2004); p.99: Nigel Wheale for 'Curlew Glide' from Flows and Traces (2003); p.41: John Wilkinson for an extract from an article by him in *Poetry Review*, Summer (2003); p.78: Worple Press for Anthony Wilson 'Prac Crit' from *Full Stretch* (2006)